A WEB OF SORROW

A WEB OF SORROW
Mistrust, Jealousy, Lovelessness, Shamelessness, Regret, and Hopelessness

Salman Akhtar

KARNAC

First published in 2017 by
Karnac Books Ltd
118 Finchley Road
London NW3 5HT

Chapters 1, 4, and 6 are reprinted with the author's and publisher's permission from: *Mistrust: Developmental, Cultural, and Clinical Realms*, ed. S. Akhtar, pp. 41–58, London: Karnac Books; *Shame: Developmental, Cultural, and Clinical Realms*, ed. S. Akhtar, pp. 93–113, London: Karnac Books, and *Hopelessness: Developmental, Cultural, and Clinical Realms*, eds. S. Akhtar and M. K. O'Neil, pp. 3–19, London: Karnac, respectively.

British Library Cataloguing in Publication Data

A C.I.P. for this book is available from the British Library

ISBN-13: 978-1-78220-566-1

Typeset by Medlar Publishing Solutions Pvt Ltd, India

Printed in Great Britain TJ International Ltd, Padstow, Cornwall

www.karnacbooks.com

To

SHANTANU & RACHANA MAITRA

in friendship

CONTENTS

PART II: SORROW FELT TO BE EMANATING
FROM INSIDE

ACKNOWLEDGEMENTS

Besides my patients from whom I have learned much about the human condition, I am grateful to many colleagues who have helped me in subtle and not-so-subtle ways. Prominent among these are Drs. Aisha Abbasi, Ira Brenner, April Fallon, Lana and Ralph Fishkin, Rao Gogineni, Jaswant Guzder, Rajnish Mago, Henri Parens, Stephen Schwartz, Shahrzad Siassi, and J. Anderson Thomson, Jr. Dr. Emily Lisco located an important bibliographic reference for me. Mr. Atin Bhattacharya provided one of the Tagore poems cited in this book. Dr. Priti Shukla read portions of this book and gave useful advice. Ms. Praveena Eeturi typed the initial drafts of two chapters. My assistant, Jan Wright, prepared the manuscript of this book with her usual diligence and good humor. Oliver Rathbone and Kate Pearce at Karnac Books shepherded the project along the various phases of publication with grace and patience. Finally, I must mention Dr. Muge Alkan who "held" me in myriad ways as I labored through this project. To all these individuals, I offer my sincere thanks.

Salman Akhtar
Philadelphia, PA

Salman Akhtar, MD, is professor of psychiatry at Jefferson Medical College and a training and supervising analyst at the Psychoanalytic Center of Philadelphia. He has served on the editorial boards of the *International Journal of Psychoanalysis*, the *Journal of the American Psychoanalytic Association*, and the *Psychoanalytic Quarterly*. His more than 300 publications include eighty-two books, of which the following seventeen are solo-authored: *Broken Structures* (1992), *Quest for Answers* (1995), *Inner Torment* (1999), *Immigration and Identity* (1999), *New Clinical Realms* (2003), *Objects of Our Desire* (2005), *Regarding Others* (2007), *Turning Points in Dynamic Psychotherapy* (2009), *The Damaged Core* (2009), *Comprehensive Dictionary of Psychoanalysis* (2009), *Immigration and Acculturation* (2011), *Matters of Life and Death* (2011), *The Book of Emotions* (2012), *Psychoanalytic Listening* (2013), *Good Stuff* (2013), *Sources of Suffering* (2014), and *No Holds Barred* (2016). Dr. Akhtar has delivered many prestigious invited lectures including a plenary address at the 2nd International Congress of the International Society for the Study of Personality Disorders in Oslo, Norway (1991), an invited plenary paper at the 2nd International Margaret S. Mahler Symposium in Cologne, Germany (1993), an invited plenary paper at the Rencontre Franco-Americaine de Psychanalyse meeting in Paris, France (1994), a keynote address at the 43rd IPA Congress in Rio de Janeiro, Brazil (2005), the plenary address at the 150th Freud Birthday Celebration sponsored by the Dutch Psychoanalytic Society and the Embassy of Austria in Leiden, Holland (2006), and the inaugural address at the first IPA-Asia Congress in Beijing, China (2010). Dr. Akhtar is the recipient of numerous awards including the American Psychoanalytic Association's Edith Sabshin Award (2000), Columbia University's Robert Liebert Award for Distinguished Contributions to Applied Psychoanalysis (2004), the American Psychiatric Association's Kun Po Soo Award (2004) and Irma Bland Award for being the outstanding teacher of psychiatric residents in the country (2005). He received the highly prestigious Sigourney Award (2012) for distinguished contributions to psychoanalysis. In 2103, he gave the commencement address at graduation ceremonies of the Smith College School of Social Work in Northampton, MA. Dr. Akhtar's books have been translated in many languages, including German, Italian, Korean, Romanian, Serbian, Spanish, and Turkish. A true Renaissance man, Dr. Akhtar has served as the film review editor for the *International Journal of Psychoanalysis*, and is currently serving as the book review editor for the *International Journal of Applied Psychoanalytic Studies*. He has published nine collections of poetry and serves as a scholar-in-residence at the Inter-Act Theatre Company in Philadelphia.

Whither sorrow?

Dictionaries define "sorrow" as a feeling of deep distress caused by loss, disappointment, or other misfortune suffered by oneself or others. However, they note a sharp decline in the use of the word "sorrow." Nobody feels sorrow anymore, it seems. In fact, upon being asked when was the last time they uttered the word, colleagues and friends simply scratched their heads. Proficient in English though they were, the word "sorrow" had not adorned (or, shall we say, pierced) their tongue in many years. Some had never used it.

So should we conclude that our world is now "sorrow-free"? Clearly this is not the case. One does not have to see the faces of staring African children that various aid agencies deploy in their television fund-raising appeals to know that sorrow exists. No trip to filth-laden shanty towns of India, war-torn regions of Syria and Iraq, and refugee camps scattered like small pox pustules all over the world is needed to know that sorrow exists. And, it exists in less dramatic forms too. A young mother whose rheumatoid arthritis does not permit her to play with her child, an athlete who has become quadriplegic as a result of a car accident, and an academician with rapidly worsening Alzheimer's—all give testimony to sorrow, both within themselves and in the hearts of those who care for them.

Still finer grains of sorrow are to be found in moments of realization that grown-up children have stopped calling our house "home," or when a novel that had captured our hearts and minds for the past few weeks comes to an end, or when we become aware that our capacity to make new friends has dried up. And, to top it all, there is sorrow at aging. Each new wrinkle, each crack in the surface of fingernails, each hesitation before strenuous physical activity, loss of physical and sexual stamina, illness and death of friends, and fear that one is uttering platitudes all the time and has become a bit boring not only to others but to oneself as well—brings sorrow to the threshold of the heart.

Given the such ubiquitous presence of sorrow, its disappearance from linguistic exchange is surprising indeed. Could it be that in this era of specialization, people speak only of components and catalysts of sorrow? Of loss of hope, of lack of love, of decline of fidelity, or of regret? And, if so, then that's where we need to begin. In a piecemeal and even "scientific manner," deal with topics like mistrust, jealousy, lovelessness, regret, and so on. We must realize, though, that tackling such component scenarios is but one way of talking about the sadness that underlies them all. And, that in the end, we shall come full circle back to sorrow itself. Let us see.

PART I

SORROW FELT TO BE EMANATING FROM OUTSIDE

CHAPTER ONE

Mistrust

The capacity to have confidence in oneself and to trust others develops during infancy and early childhood. However, experiences during later childhood and adolescence also modulate and refine these attributes. Adulthood too involves transactions (e.g., in the course of developing romantic intimacy, entering into a marital contract, buying or selling a house, and relying upon the health-care system during old age) which test the balance between trust and mistrust, confidence and timidity, and gullibility and inordinate caution. Such challenges of adult life to the trust-mistrust economy form the topic of this contribution. Before delving into them and into the clinical management of mistrustful adult patients, however, it seems useful to quickly review the psychoanalytic literature on the ontogenesis of trust and mistrust.

Childhood foundations of trust and mistrust

Contemporary psychoanalysis has firmly rejected Freud's (1911c) early notion that mistrustful and paranoid traits of personality evolved from the repudiation of latent homosexuality through projection. This formulation was found untenable on the grounds that it (i) failed to account for paranoid traits in individuals who were overtly and comfortably homosexual, (ii) overemphasized the role of libido over aggression in the genesis of paranoid hostility, and (iii) ignored the actual harshness faced by the paranoid individual while growing up. Such repudiation of Freud's proposal makes perfect sense.

To Freud's credit, however, it should be noted that in subsequent writings, he included three other factors in the genesis of paranoid tendencies. These were (i) actual early experiences of threat to survival (1922b), (ii) constitutional excess of aggression in temperament (1923b), and (iii) marked anger towards the mother during the preoedipal phase of development (1933a). This line of Freud's thinking was elaborated upon by Klein (1946), who held that the earliest orientation of the infant to the world is essentially paranoid: inner aggression is externalized and the resulting persecutory anxiety is defended by splitting (which keeps the "good" and "bad" objects apart), denial (which masks the fact that one needs objects to survive), and primitive idealization (which fuels fantasies of unlimited gratification from "good" objects). The individual who gets fixated on this position remains vulnerable to grandiosity, contempt, and mistrust of others. Advance from such "paranoid position" to "depressive position" (that permits humility, mourning, gratitude, and reparation) is a result of greater drive-integration.

In contrast, Winnicott (1952) emphasized the role of external environment in the genesis of mistrust. He posited that the infant experiences any interference with his "going-on-being" as a menace. The end of intrauterine bliss, with birth, provides the deepest template for such disturbances. However, the mother's devoted care neutralizes the resulting inchoate anxiety. A rudimentary yet authentic self begins to come into its own. For this to continue, however, the mother not only has to satisfy the infant's needs but also must provide an unobtrusive presence in the background from which the infant can gather bits and pieces of his personal experience. Maternal failures in either regard lead to disruption of the infant's being. Anxiety, inner withdrawal, and diminution of psychic freedom follow. Later, such a child displays lack of playfulness, motor stiffness, and preoccupation with fantasies of cruelty. With the onset of adolescence, social isolation, disturbing persecutory dreams, and overt suspiciousness are added to the clinical picture.

Erikson (1950) also posited that paranoid trends had their genesis in overwhelming frustrations during early infancy, which impede the development of "basic trust." Instead, there develops a lack of confidence, followed by increasing helplessness, pessimism, and feelings of shame and doubt. The subsequent history is punctuated by rigid morality, inhibition of spontaneity, deterioration of peer relationships, development of omnipotent fantasies to mask inner inferiority, and ultimately the syndrome of "identity diffusion" (see also Akhtar, 1984), with a mixture of negativism, self-isolation, and avoidance of intimacy with others.

To those pioneering observations (by Freud, Klein, Winnicott, and Erikson), later psychoanalysts added nuances. Rycroft (1960), for instance, noted that the paranoid individual's pretensions to genius compensate for the lack of object love in his life. Isaacs, Alexander, and Haggard (1963) emphasized that parental forthrightness in dealings with their child exerts a powerful impact on the child's developing sense of trust. Identification with parents who are consistent and reliable leads to the development of trustworthiness in the child. However, exposure to parents who misuse a child's trust in them causes great hurt and disillusionment. Under such circumstances:

> A disillusionment occurs which is a great blow to the psyche. If the child has a strong enough ego, he will integrate the fact as a determinant of limitations and restrictions on the trustworthiness of parents and others. If he has a somewhat weaker ego, the disappointment may connote a loss of the illusion of ideal parent and thereby mean a resulting anger—the distrust may be repressed, and leave the child unprepared to discriminate between trustworthy and untrustworthy persons. He has thereby become gullible, for he can only indiscriminately trust. (p. 464)[1]

Such naïveté can coexist, in a split-off manner, with suspiciousness. Shapiro (1965), who delineated the characteristics of paranoid cognition in detail, emphasized this while also noting the paranoid person's mental rigidity, disregard of new data, intolerance of ambiguity, and the constant search for clues that confirm a preexisting bias. Jacobson (1971) observed that paranoid individuals had frequently grown up in families where there was overt cruelty and much bickering between parents. A markedly sadomasochistic family atmosphere, often focusing on a parent's marital infidelity, sets the stage for the development of the child's own sadism. Severe early frustrations prevent the building up of unambivalent object relations and stable identifications. The child's self-esteem is weakened, and there develops a sense of futility about finding love in the future. Kernberg (1984) noted that while paranoid and narcissistic preconditions can coexist, in general, paranoid individuals are aloof and suspicious and not envious and exploitative like the narcissists.

Mention must also be made of Blum's (1980, 1981) papers, which masterfully synthesize the classic and contemporary psychoanalytic writings on paranoia. According to Blum, hostility is a primary problem in this condition and not merely a defense. A complex interplay of innate disposition, actual threats to survival during childhood, impaired object relations, and subsequent structural defects and defensive elaborations underlie the ultimate paranoid picture in adulthood. Interweaving his propositions with Mahler, Pine, and Bergman's (1975) theory of separation–individuation, Blum pointed out that the lack of internalization of the comforting mother is associated with a lack of ego integration, untamed infantile omnipotence, fragile self-esteem, and a tendency toward intense separation anxiety. In this context, Blum (1981) introduced his concept of "inconstant object," the ambivalently loved object that is felt to be both persecutory and needed. Such an object cannot be allowed to have an independent existence. The threat of betrayal must be tenaciously maintained. The ever-present fear of persecution then becomes the reciprocal of libidinal object constancy and a desperate effort to preserve a "reliable" object. However, as Weigert (1959) stated long ago:

> The lonely person may learn to channel the rage of frustration into skillful manipulations by which he handles men like things, forcing them to grant compensations for the despair of loneliness. Such compulsive manipulations remain unsatisfactory. Only a relation of trust grants the freedom to arrive at a creative integration of needs. It implies a daring risk, it does not enforce gratifications, since no amount of enforced gratification of isolated needs in a lonely individual can substitute for the over-all sense of confirmed existence which arises from a relation of trust that makes the child—and later the adult—at home in a world that surrounds Being with the horrors of Non-being. (p. 33)

Weigert thus underscored the importance of trust in others and also in one's own ability to tolerate frustrations, separations, and losses without despair. Along with the literature summarized above, this lays the groundwork for considering how the developmental tasks of adult life (see Akhtar, 2009a, for a concise summary) are facilitated by a solid capacity for trust. In turn, the feeling of trust is strengthened by efficacy in handling such tasks. However, Neri (2005) wisely reminds us that:

> The stabilization of trust, then, cannot just depend upon the reliability of our relationships, but must also be based on an increase in our capacity to cope with the uncertainty of relationships, relying on our own sense of security (self-esteem). The stabilization of trust, in other words, depends also on the resources we have available to "neutralize" disappointments; that is, to consider them as the effect of our human limitations, of a simple mistake, of an unfortunate coincidence, and not as the effect of, for instance, our friends' betrayal or deliberate attempts to hurt us; or, perhaps, as the result of our own unworthiness. To learn to neutralize disappointments is not at all an indifferent achievement. It means that, whenever we are confronted with what makes us feel disappointed, we have to learn to employ a different interpretative grid from the ones we had utilized on previous occasions. If we can rely on a certain amount of inner security, on intrinsic self-trust, this will allow us to believe that we can find a way out from whatever situation in which we find ourselves. (p. 86)

That being said, we are now prepared to plunge into the specific developmental tasks of adulthood and explicate their dialectical relationship with trust in oneself and others.

Issues of trust and mistrust during adulthood

The complex and multifaceted tasks of adult life test one's capacity to trust others and to retain self-confidence. During early adult years, four important psychosocial tasks arise: (i) forming a "dream" for oneself and giving it a place in the life narrative, (ii) finding a mentor, (iii) making a vocational choice, and (iv) establishing a mature love relationship (Levinson, Darrow, Klein, Levinson, & McKee, 1978). Then come the trials and tribulations of marriage, parenthood, and child-rearing. Following this, the arrival of middle age forces an encounter with limits of acquisition, achievement, and creativity. Shifts also happen in one's relationship with one's parents and with one's children. Thoughts of retirement begin to surface and are followed by their actualization. Life changes. Time enters the subjective experience in a sharp way. More of life is felt to be gone and less left. Soon one finds oneself getting old, with all the attendant physical and social anxieties of this life era. Moreover, there is the existential necessity to develop a deep and post-ambivalent view of the world that one has lived in and is about to leave. As can be readily seen, issues of trust and mistrust are frequently activated by all the foregoing developmental epochs. Brief comments on each of these phases now follow.

Work and job

Establishing a career trajectory is an important and necessary task of young adulthood. However, both choosing and building a career are complex tasks involving encounters with new situations and unknown outcomes. Many careers necessitate the development of new skills and require faith, long-term hard work, and not a little luck to achieve success. In all aforementioned respects, careers call on young adults to display a remarkable amount of trust in themselves and other people.

The choice of where to begin one's career involves trust in one's ability to realistically assess one's talents, understand and engage the world, and finally strike out on one's own (Lidz, 1968). It also usually means relying upon varying mentors, large and small, who illuminate one's intended path. The mentor not only gives the younger adult a sense of the world she intends to enter but also illustrates the kind of person the young adult should aspire to become.[2]

Once settled in the workplace, the young adult must form productive bonds with coworkers and "bosses." The ecosystem of the workplace becomes an extended social network. Just as trust permeates networks that brings people together, it must also be found in the workplace among coworkers. A young adult can build the reputation for being "trustworthy" when he or she follows through on tasks. As the career progresses, reliance upon seniors diminishes and the need to outsource tasks to others arises; this requires an ability to trust that one's subordinates will indeed finish the tasks assigned to them. Interestingly, a degree of trust must often be present in society at large to enable proper engagement with a career. Unstable political societies often breed distrust and lack of motivation. If people cannot trust that their work will have expected and good consequences, they often disengage and become indifferent. Indeed, no young adult builds an exciting career without knowing that success is an achievable and worthy goal. Such "confident expectation" (Benedek, 1938) is drawn from gratifying childhood experiences and is nurtured by the reassuring political and economic realities of the organization one works for. Sievers (2003) emphasizes that when organizations tend to engineer trust by the means of institutional audits and procedures, they end up generating mistrust. True trust in the workplace depends upon both the trustworthiness of workers themselves and the capacity of their leaders to hear their complaints and accept genuine differences of opinion without reprisals.

Love and marriage

Finding a mate can occupy a large swath of young adulthood. It is never a straight path and takes considerable time, often with many hassles, hiccups, and heartbreaks. This is especially true now that few marriages are "arranged." The absence of the external facilitation means that young adults have to find and choose a partner based on their own instincts and desires. This process usually entails dating, which requires a considerable degree of trust both in oneself and other people. There is inherent uncertainty to this situation. Not being married, two people do not have any explicit or permanent loyalty to one another. The ties between them are ephemeral and only a rare date leads to marriage. Most end with disappointment and yet young adults continue to date. They do so because they want to meet someone, and because it is enjoyable; their capacity to trust another person enables them to persevere. For instance, when a date is decided upon, a person trusts the other person will show up and behave in a respectful and appropriate manner. If the relationship progresses and the two individuals become intimate, they begin to place increasing amounts of trust in each other. They trust that the other person cares for them and will treat them with an amount of consideration that goes beyond what is expected from an acquaintance or friend.

When dating leads to engagement, a whole new set of tasks that require trust enter a young person's life. Planning a wedding introduces issues that need to be resolved within a couple. Take the wedding ceremony. The young couple may come from different religious backgrounds and while they may be secular-minded themselves, their parents can be of a different mindset. Other issues such as location and size of wedding can introduce differences between the couple and their respective families. One family can be more traditional and want a religious ceremony followed by a formal reception while the other family is more bohemian and sees the wedding happening in a more simple setting. Other points of contention can be introduced by the sudden awareness that a future mother-in-law is going to be much more involved than was previously counted on. All these issues must be resolved between the couple through discussion and compromise, a process that is much aided by mutual trust and respect.

After the wedding comes the reality of married life, with its own challenges and pleasures. Young married couples can be heard the world over saying that the first year of marriage is often the most difficult. This sentiment gives voice to the fact that the reality of marital partnership is quite different from courtship. Now the two individuals must abide by the mutually shared goals of a family. The merging process within marriage is challenging and greatly aided by mutual trust between partners (Akhtar & Billinkoff, 2011). As young adults, they have recently mastered autonomy (from the family of origin) and yet must now withdraw a little from the position of total autonomy. Losing autonomy is healthy and good for a relationship but can be scary for an individual. The partners must have faith in the good intentions of each other. Less obvious is the need for trust in the future. They must trust that in the evolving years of life, they will change in ways that are generally beneficial and pleasant for their relationship.

Clearly, things do not always go smoothly. Unmanageable tensions can arise between marital partners, due to all sorts of reasons. The most common of them include financial disagreements, influence of other family members, and real or alleged infidelity. Under fortunate circumstances, such conflicts can be worked through with the help of some professional intervention. Matters can get worse, however. All trust between the partners is now destroyed. They might end up seeking separation and divorce. Ideally, a modicum of interpersonal trust can be maintained and self-confidence of the two partners is not eroded to a malignant extent. Unfortunately, this is not always the case (Ehrlich, 2014; Wallerstein, Lewis, & Blakeslee, 2000).

Parenthood and child-rearing

Trust in oneself, in one's partner, and in the overall functioning of the couple is essential for the decision to become a parent and to select the timing for such a life change. Significant shifts then follow in the couple's work life, economic potential, and erotic availability to each other. Negotiating the ebb and flow of emotions that are unleashed as a result requires mutual trust and love. The same applies to the challenges of child rearing from infancy to adolescence. These too require the partners in a couple to take each other seriously, respect their different approaches, and find satisfactory compromises.

However, the tasks involved in child rearing cannot be separated from the overall functioning of the family. Nothing that happens within a family remains an isolated event. Open communication and mutual respect is the key to a harmonious family atmosphere. Jaques's (2005) resounding statement below says it all:

> A family whose members cannot and do not trust each other, whose members would lie to each other, or do injury to each other, whose parental figures are not truly and reliably betrothed, turns an abode into a social nightmare. Family members do not necessarily all have to love each other. But, regardless of unevenness in love among them, trust must be ensured. Suspicion and mistrust are death to a family. (p. 397)

One realm of family life where the necessity of all members (father, mother, brother, sister) to trust each other is of paramount importance involves maintenance of proper boundaries. Each "healthy" or "healthy enough" family respects the demarcation between the parent–child and male–female categories. As a consequence, some activities, some functions, some things, and some spaces within the family's dwelling place belong to parents and others to children. Likewise, some of the above-mentioned objects and actions belong to males and the others to females of the family. Both parent–child and male–female divisions of this sort are not absolute. Overlaps and admixtures exist. Nonetheless, at extremes, a certain separation is maintained. And, it is taken for granted that violations of limits and boundaries will not occur. This requires the family members to have trust in each other.

Midlife and retirement

As the individual arrives at the threshold of midlife (around fifty to fifty-five years of age), he begins to sense that there are limits to what he can achieve or do in this world. The allure of material acquisitions (e.g., a better car, a bigger house) which he fervently pursued during his youth now begins to wane. More can no longer be acquired or can only be acquired at a huge cost on some other front; it therefore seems less appealing. In the intellectual and creative realms, too, one begins to notice the limits of one's vision and capability. Wishful self-representations, which one thought would be realized "someday" (Akhtar, 1996), reveal their illusory nature. The physician who held onto the fantasy of acquiring a law degree in the future now finds that he has to let go of that idea. The school teacher who always wanted to enter active politics but kept postponing it realizes during middle or late middle age that it is too late to get on a party bandwagon.

Limits also appear in other realms. The body undergoes change and slowly begins to lose its agility and strength. Physical appearance and sexual functioning are affected, often with significant emotional consequences. There also develops an increasing awareness, during middle age, of the psychic separateness of one's children and of the limited control (and even access) one has over their evolving emotional and social life. One is forced by necessity to alter one's own parental self-representation as children enter adolescence and disengage from the life at home in favor of life with peers and life in the world at large.

One's sense of the passage of time is also affected. Months and years seem to fly by. One can no longer multiply one's age by two and remain convinced that one would still be alive. Consequently, one concludes that more of one's life is behind and less is left to live. Middle age thus causes an uncanny shift in the individual's perspective of time. The inherent transience of all relationships becomes undeniable.

> Even the stability of the inanimate world now seems threatened: the cities one knows from the past change, neighborhoods change, and these external changes may symbolize and reinforce all mourning processes regarding loss and separation. The awareness of the ephemerality of human life becomes a very concrete and powerful force which increases mourning processes—and growth connected with them—and fosters an orientation to both the past that is gone and the future that now seems nearer …. To accept oneself within such limits is an important aspect of emotional maturity that is in contrast to narcissistic rationalization, to denial, to resignation and cynicism, and to masochistic self blame. (Kernberg, 1980, pp. 126–127)

Middle age thus brings compromised physical strength, diminished omnipotence, reduction in the time one is allotted to live, and significant decrease of authority over children. The last-mentioned feeling increases dramatically when the latter find love and get married. The resulting expansion of the family roster tests the nuances of trust; what can be shared with "new family members" and what must remain within the family of origin now becomes a matter of consideration. Two other areas that put self-confidence to test are (i) the subtle shifts in the inherently bisexual nature of identity, and (ii) retirement from one's job. The midlife transformation of identity was first commented upon by Jung (1933), who wrote that:

> We might compare masculinity and femininity to a particular store of substances of which, in the first half of life, unequal use is made. A man consumes his large supply of masculine substance, and has left over only the smaller amount of feminine substance, which he must now put to use. It is the other way around with a woman: she allows her unused supply of masculinity to become more active. (p. 107)

To manifest the behavioral changes associated with such intrapsychic shifts, one needs a great amount of self-confidence and a comparable degree of trust in one's partner's capacity to accept this reality.

The other challenge is retirement from one's job. This involves the loss of a significant network of relationships. The social sphere in which one takes part shrinks. The subsequent isolation coupled with the absence of daily confirmations of efficacy can lead to a crisis of self-esteem (Pollock, 1971). Having to forge newer outlets of energy, including those related to internet websites, and find new avenues of relatedness (via Facebook, Twitter, etc.) helps to a certain extent. However, it also has the potential of exposing "unmentalized xenophobia" (Akhtar, 2007), and hitherto covert mistrust of others. Finding efficacy and enjoyment after freedom from the humdrum of daily employment, on the other hand, can bring forth hidden strength and enhance self-confidence (Borchard, 2006).

Old age and infirmity

Old age is frequently associated with encountering the deaths of friends and siblings, leaving one wistful and alone. Physical limitations of greater or lesser degree appear and enhance the need to depend upon others. One begins to long for unconditional love all over again, that is, the sort of love only the mother of early childhood can provide. However, the childlike relaxation that comes with this longing can only be expressed in deeply trusted relationships. Even the reminiscences of childhood and youth can only be shared with long-term associates and spouses of long-term duration.

As the elderly witness the passing of their contemporaries and the senescence of their bodies, they sense the approach of their own deaths more clearly. At this point, "death anxiety" or what Freud (1923b, p. 58) called *Todesangst* can emerge, often to the extent that it overwhelms the ego. From the early writings of Freud through Eissler's (1955) important paper on the topic to the views of contemporary analysts (Fayek, 1981; Langs, 2004)[3], feeling anxious about dying has been taken for granted. However, this might not always be true. Not only is there a disagreement between Western and Eastern perspectives on death in this regard (Akhtar, 2010, 2011b), differences also exist between Western philosophers themselves with some arguing for death being always unwelcome and frightening and others proposing that death can bring relief and even peace (for an eloquent meditation on such divergences, see Barnes, 2008). Within psychoanalysis, too, an unrecognized minority (Akhtar, 2011b; Weissman, 1972; Wheelis, 1971) question the ubiquitous nature of death anxiety and propose that an "appropriate" death does not cause such distress. I think that the psychoanalytic literature on emotional reactions to death has failed to distinguish between a premature, unexpected, and violent death and a timely, expectable, and natural death. And, this conflation has resulted in the stance that "death anxiety" is ubiquitous. The fact, most likely, is that the thought of premature death (which arises out of our own unmitigated destructiveness) does cause anxiety and the thought of expected death (which arises out of acceptance of reality and from our capacity for contentment) does not cause anxiety.

When the elderly accept the reality of death, they start to gently prepare themselves for their passing. This involves anticipatory mourning for the final separation from loved ones as well as the inner consolidation of a genuinely post-ambivalent worldview (Akhtar, 1994). Forgiving oneself for mistakes made and forgiving others for their limitations constitutes another important task at this point. The attempt is to meet what the renowned thanatologist, Edwin Shneidman (2008), called a "good-enough death." Such a death is:

> ... appropriate to the individual's time of life, to his style of life, to his situation in life, to his mission (aspirations, goals, wishes) in life; and it is appropriate to the significant others in his life. Obviously, what is appropriate differs from person to person: one man's nemesis is another man's passion. Appropriateness has many dimensions, relating, at the least, to the state of one's health, competence, energy, prowess, zeal, hope, pain, and investment in his post-self. (p. 19)[4]

On a plebeian level, the elderly face decisions regarding disbursing their material possessions and regarding how their bodily selves will be disposed of after death. Trusting that others will indeed carry out their wishes brings a sense of peace and mastery over one's life.

Pertinent psychiatric syndromes

In general, the issues of trust and mistrust that draw the attention of a psychoanalyst or psychotherapist are mild. Selecting cases that are "analyzable" (or at least seem to be so) filters more serious and intractable problems of mistrust though occasional surprises do occur; this becomes strikingly evident when the analyst discovers that the patient has been lying to him all along during his treatment. Before addressing the dilemmas of technique with such patients, a brief comment upon severe paranoid conditions that are the purview of general psychiatrists (but can show up at the psychoanalyst's threshold as well) seems to be in order.

This spectrum begins with a firmly ensconced paranoid personality disorder whose manifestations can be grouped under the following six categories (Akhtar, 1990):

- *Self-concept*: paranoid individuals have a hidden core of timidity and fear against which they evolve an intimidating, grandiose, and unduly formal self. Scornful and contemptuous of others, they can become easily enraged.
- *Interpersonal relations*: their relationships are characterized by suspiciousness, aloofness, and vigilance. At the same time, they can be

surprisingly naïve and gullible, with a special vulnerability to believe in gossip (Stanton, 1978). They lack a sense of humor and are averse to physical overtures of intimacy. Unable to be content with "good-enough revenge" (Akhtar, 2014a), they hold long-term grudges and tend to be quite vindictive.

- *Social adaptation*: Their industrious, cautious, and driven attitude might lead to success in solitary, critical lines of work. However, they have frequent difficulties with coworkers, and possess little capacity to enjoy "softer" pleasures of life, such as poetry.

- *Love and sexuality*: This is another area of tension for such individuals. On the surface, they appear devoid of romantic interests and capabilities. Underneath such dry persona, they carry a vulnerability to erotomania and sadomasochistic perversions.

- *Ethics, standards, and ideals*: While insisting for others to be forever truthful, individuals with paranoid personalities tend to lie themselves. Tobak (1989) has especially delineated the frequent coexistence of an expedient mendacity with moralistic self-righteousness in the paranoid character.

- *Cognitive style*: They display sharp attention, oratorical skills, and tendency towards argumentation and perceptual hair-splitting (Shapiro, 1965). However, "narrow-mindedness" (Brenman, 1985) prevents them from grasping the "big picture." Proud of their pursuit of truth, they frequently fail to see the "whole truth."

More severe conditions than this also exist. These include (i) reactive development of paranoid delusions, (ii) paranoia or "delusional disorder", and (iii) paranoid schizophrenia. The *first* condition is generally seen among individuals who have experienced drastic changes in their environment, such as fresh immigrants, refugees, prisoners of war, inductees into military services, and, at times, even young people leaving their homes for the first time to attend college. The delusions among such individuals are "comprehensible" (in the context of their circumstances) and rarely become chronic. Provision of empathy, relatively basic reconstructive interventions, and establishment of safe "holding" (Winnicott, 1960a, 1960b) structures tend to bring them back to contact with consensual reality. The *second* condition is paranoia or the so-called "delusional disorder." Akin to paranoid personality disorder in their ego-syntonicity, chronicity, and relatively encapsulated nature, the mistrustful beliefs of paranoia are farther removed from reality (Winokur, 1977) and more tenaciously held. The *third* condition is paranoid schizophrenia. Here the break with reality is readily evident to all who come in contact with the individual. The individual suffering from this condition displays bizarre and fixed notions of persecution, grandiosity, and jealousy or infidelity. The clinical picture also consists of auditory hallucinations, experiences of thought control, incongruous affect, and gross peculiarities of behavior in the form of social withdrawal or violent attacks against others. This disorder is not amenable to psychotherapy; it requires psychopharmacological management, hospitalization, and supportive long-term rehabilitative care. Paradoxically, this very comment brings up the fact that "milder" forms of mistrust and suspiciousness can indeed be handled by means of psychotherapy and psychoanalysis, though occasionally some special interventions might have to be utilized. Before entering into a discussion of such matters, I would like to make a brief foray into the sociocultural realm as it involves matters of trust and mistrust.

Sociocultural aspects

Trust plays a major role in the proper functioning of a society. The Nobel laureate Amartya Sen (1999) emphasizes that "transparency guarantees" (p. 38) enhanced mutual trust between group members and this, in turn, forms an important scaffold for each member's personal freedom. Sen declares that:

> In social interactions, individuals deal with one another on the basis of some presumption of what they are being offered and what they can expect to get. In this sense, the society operates on some basic presumption of trust. *Transparency guarantees* deal with the need for openness that people can expect: the freedom to deal with one another under guarantees of disclosure and lucidity. When that trust is seriously violated, the lives of many people—both direct parties and third parties—may be adversely affected by the lack of openness. Transparency guarantees (including the right to disclosure) can thus be an important category of instrumental freedom. These guarantees have a clear instrumental role in preventing corruption, financial irresponsibility and underhand dealings. (pp. 39–40, italics in the original)

There might exist additional variables that enhance trust in a given social structure and such variables might vary across cultures. In discussing trust-building across cultures, Asherman, Bing, and Laroche (2000) note that in China and many Arab and Latin American countries, building relationships is a prerequisite for professional collaboration. Thus, one has to expose one's personal life to a greater extent that one does in the United States and one has to listen to personal details of those whom one is going to work with; trust is both needed for it and gets strengthened by such exchange. Yuki, Maddux, Brewer, and Takemura (2005) found that Americans tend to trust in-group members more than out-group members whereas Japanese allocate trust based upon shared direct or indirect interpersonal links. And, Indians trust authority figures instinctively and to a greater extent than do Americans (Roland, 1988).

Such cultural variations most likely arise from varying patterns of child-rearing. Societies with joint and extended families and "we-selves" (Roland, 1988) offer prolonged symbiotic luxuriance to a child, who is pretty much never alone, and thus encourage trust in collective opinion, family, and those akin to familial idiom. Societies which encourage the child's separateness, autonomy, and self-reliance from quite early on tend to enhance self-confidence at the cost of diminishing trust in others. The prevalence of crime, violence, child seduction, and pedophilia in a given society also propels parents to teach their children not to trust strangers, an injunction that seems quite foreign to most parents in Asia.

Clearly, psychological traits and capacities derived from childhood experience with parents get reinforced (or dissipated) by the social institutions the child encounters during his or her growth. Erikson (1950) made this clear when he wrote the following:

> The parental faith which supports the trust emerging in the newborn, has throughout history sought its institutional safeguard (and, on occasion, found its greatest enemy) in organized religion. Trust born of care is, in fact, the touchstone of the *actuality* of a given religion. All religions have in common the periodical childlike surrender to a Provider or providers who dispense earthly fortune as well as spiritual health; some demonstration of man's smallness by way of reduced posture and humble gesture; the admission in prayer and song of misdeeds, of misthoughts, and of evil intentions;

fervent appeal for inner unification by divine guidance; and finally, the insight that individual trust must become a common faith. (p. 250, italics in the original)

Putting all this together, one may safely draw five conclusions about the relationship between trust and culture: (i) mutual trust is essential for cultural coherence; (ii) transparency of social transactions and governmental practices enhances trust;[5] (iii) modal child rearing practices can determine the extent and form of trust; (iv) the developmentally derived trust is affected (sustained, enhanced, or damaged) by societal institutions, and (v) the variables listed above act in a silent and cumulative unison. Having thus put sociocultural matters regarding trust in a nutshell, we can now turn our attention to clinical concerns.

Implications for conducting psychotherapy and psychoanalysis

Facilitating the development of trust on the part of a new patient— someone the therapist is meeting for the first time in his or her life—is an important early task in clinical work. Assuming that the patient possesses "a fairly reliable character" (Freud, 1905a, p. 263) and does not carry an extra quantum of suspiciousness, helping him to trust the therapist poses little difficulty. The therapist's punctuality, reliability in keeping appointments, warmth, and sustained concern evoke the patient's trust. Encountering a person (the therapist) who listens, explains, and is related in an authentic and non-defensive manner enhances the patient's faith in the process that is beginning to unfold (R. Levin, 1998; Meissner, 1969). One particular area in which such forthrightness is of special importance from the very first contact between the therapist and patient involves the latter's questions about the treatment being recommended. The therapist should answer them factually and not derail or mystify the patient by "interpreting" the reasons behind his questions. For instance, the patient may frequently ask about the difference between psychoanalysis and psychotherapy. Subtle controversies in the field notwithstanding, it is possible to answer this question in a simple, straightforward way. One might explain the difference not only in terms of frequency of visits and the use of the couch but, to a certain extent, in terms of the nature of the patient's expected role and the therapist's stance vis-à-vis the patient's report of his thoughts, feelings, fantasies, and dreams.

Another area of frequent concern to patients, especially in this era of consumerism, is their psychiatric diagnosis. Exploring the patient's reasons for asking this might reveal further significant information. However, such exploration should not be used as delay tactics, and a patient who wants to know his diagnosis should be told. Much is made of a patient's misunderstanding of diagnostic terminology or being narcissistically injured by it. What is overlooked is that the interviewer's cryptic attitude, fudging, and uncomfortable avoidance, too, can have alienating and adverse effects on the patient.

Handling matters in such a clinically forthright manner goes a long way in establishing trust between the therapist and the patient. Matters can get complicated all over again though once the treatment gets going. Gently empathizing with the patient's hesitation in revealing this or that "unacceptable" or "bad" thought or feeling is the first step in resolving such difficulty. Soon, however, the interventions must revert to the customary measures of "defense analysis" (Brenner, 1976; Fenichel, 1941; A. Freud, 1936; Ross, 2003), that is, unmasking the ego's attempts to ward-off anxiety (aroused by resurgent wishes) in the here-and-now of the clinical situation. All this applies to milder, "neurotic," and transient mistrust. There are instances, however, where the patients' inability or unwillingness to trust is more intractable. Two transference developments prove to be especially challenging.

In the first, the patient comes regularly, pays bills on time, and seems to be abiding by the "fundamental rule" (Freud, 1900a), but in actuality, is consistently lying to the therapist and withholding useful information. The patient in such "psychopathic transference" (Kernberg, 1992) often tries "unconsciously to provoke the therapist to deceptive or dishonest behavior, or at least to inconsistencies in his behavior that the patient may then interpret as dishonesty" (p. 223). Kernberg (1992) proposes that the proper approach under such circumstances is to confront the patient tactfully but directly and to explore the inherent transference relationship in detail and to resolve it interpretively before proceeding with other issues. Typically, the "psychopathic transference" gets transformed into "paranoid transference" before giving way to depressive reparative feelings and genuine self-concern.

Paranoid transference is expressed through serious distortions in the patient-therapist relationship, even to the extent of the patient developing an encapsulated psychosis. Here, the technical recommendations of Kernberg (1992) are extremely useful.

If the patient seriously distorts the reality of the therapist's behavior, the therapist tells the patient that, in his view, their realities are completely different and incompatible. Confronting the patient with these incompatible realities reproduces the situation that occurs when a "mad" person and a "normal" person try to communicate without an outside witness or arbitrator to clarify what is real. The only alternative to the existence of truly incompatible realities at that point would be that the therapist is lying to the patient; and if the patient were so convinced, that would need to be explored further. (p. 234)

When the patient's transference fears and accusations acquire a delusional quality, "… the therapist's communicating his tolerance of incompatible realities and examining fully the implications of the patient-therapist relationship under such conditions may gradually lead to the interpretive resolution of the psychotic nucleus and of the paranoid transference itself" (p. 235).

At times, the patient's beginning to trust the analyst itself becomes a source of distress and fear. This often happens because the emergence of trust is invariably accompanied by increased hope and this, in turn, also creates the possibility of disappointment and betrayal. Neri (2005) has eloquently described such an affective turn within the transference–countertransference matrix:

When the patient begins to trust, he also begins to give up that condition of detachment and perplexity (the noise, the feeling of meaninglessness of this kind of conversation) which allowed him to control his involvement and emotional distance; however, he has still not been accepted (the chance that his presence could be noticed). If there is any hope that he could be understood and helped, then there is also a chance that he could be left feeling disappointed and betrayed yet again. This possibility is truly frightening and anxiety provoking. At times, the conflict between trust and suspicion, between need and fear, is particularly dramatic. It is as if a person felt a great need to eat but at the same time was also frightened that the food could have been poisoned. Similarly, patients can feel that their analyst's words are both essential and dangerous to them. These words might save them, but might also hurt them or even put them in extreme danger. (p. 83)

The analyst must speak directly and in a lucid manner in such situations. He must demonstrate to the patient his awareness of what he is putting inside the patient's mind and how, he believes, it can affect the patient. Neri (2005) also deems it "advisable for the analyst to promote reciprocity in the relationship, [thinking that] a person feels trust for someone who trusts him" (p. 83). At the same time, however, interpretive attention should also be directed towards the all-or-none attitude of omnipotence that is hidden under the patient's mistrust and hopelessness (see Akhtar, 1996, for the analysis of the "someday ..." fantasy in this context).

It is through a judicious admixture of "holding" (Winnicott, 1960a, 1960b) and interpretive approaches and trust, too, on a sustained basis (often for months and years) that mistrustful individuals can be helped to relax and develop a trusting dependence that they have never experienced before. Needless to add, a very important role is played here by the analyst's trust in the therapeutic process and in its capacity to work through the experiences of unsafety and distrust that arise within him during clinical work. "Because the patient knows the analyst is aware of the patient's unwanted qualities, the analyst's experience of comfort and safety with the patient can convey a trusting experience that affirms the patient's sense of his or her essential goodness, personal worth, and potential" (K. Frank, 2004, p. 342).

Concluding remarks

In this contribution, I have attempted to shed light upon adult-life ramifications of the trust-mistrust dimension of the human mind. Acknowledging that the foundation of this dialectic is laid during early childhood, if not infantile experiences of drive-satisfaction, healthy attachment, and reliable "holding," I have asserted that the trust-mistrust economy can be taxed by special developments during adulthood. Developing romantic intimacy, entering into a marital contract, workplace engagement with peers, raising children and letting them go, and participating in all events and formalities of civic life can stir up conflicts between gullibility and suspiciousness. Onset of middle age, which forces an encounter with limits of achievement, and old age, which brings the awareness of one's approaching end, also test the human need to trust family, friends, and the world at large for their beneficent and care-taking abilities. A firm and resolute allegiance to the "depressive position" (Klein, 1940) with its tempered optimism and gratitude towards others is essential for a safe passage through the turmoil of midlife and aging. Forgiveness towards those who betrayed one and genuine attempts at reparation for those betrayed by oneself furthers the capacity for mourning needed at this stage. To be sure, receiving apology and reparation from those who have inflicted wounds on one's psyche as well as the opportunity to take some revenge facilitate the processes of mourning and forgiveness (Akhtar, 2002; Akhtar & Parens, 2014). Lacking this, the traumatized individual continues to hold grudges, keeps looking for "justice," and ruminates on early hurts and betrayals. The only solace then is creativity which under fortunate circumstances and given outstanding talent can transform hideous inner suffering into plaintive literature of stunning eloquence. The following short poem by the Nobel Prize-winning Indian poet Rabindranath Tagore (1861–1941) is a gem of this very sort.

> Today my voice is choked and mute is my flute.
> My world has disappeared in an evil dream.
> There with tears I ask thee:
> "Those who have poisoned thine air
> And extinguished thy light,
> Hast thou forgiven them?
> Hast thou loved them?" (1921, p. 96)[6]

CHAPTER TWO

Jealousy

I would like to begin this chapter by quoting Marcianne Blevis's (2009) highly nuanced description of the individual afflicted by jealousy. Writing with disarming eloquence, she notes that:

> The jealous person is unable to trust anything. He doubts, suspects, or imagines extraordinary scenarios of deception, waiting for the other shoe to drop. Eventually, reality catches up with his theatre of illusions and his mistaken definition of love. He can't know or guess everything. It is obvious that his lover can never become totally transparent to him. Every human being needs her privacy, her secret garden. Yet for the jealous person, this state of affairs is intolerable. He needs total control over his subjects. (p. 3)

This portrait is remarkable not only for its literary quality but also for its bringing together a number of "meta-experiences" that go with jealousy. I will discuss such experiences soon. For now, it will suffice to say that jealousy is a painful experience that is frequently encountered in social, cultural, and clinical realms of life.

My contribution here meant to highlight the nature of this phenomenon, trace its developmental origins, and explicate the therapeutic strategies for its amelioration in cases where it acquires a seriously distressing and morbid form. In order to accomplish these goals, I will first elucidate the phenomenological features of jealousy (and its absence), then conduct a comprehensive survey of psychoanalytic writings on the topic, and attempt to interweave pertinent insights from general psychology, psychiatry, and cultural anthropology. Following this, I will discuss the technical challenges in the psycho-analytic treatment of jealous individuals and conclude by making some synthesizing remarks and by pointing out areas that merit fur-ther attention.

Descriptive features

The etymology of the current English word "jealousy" is so well-traced by David Buss (2000) that paraphrasing him would simply not do. Hence, I quote him at length here.

> The word *jealousy* came into the English language through the French language. Comparable words in French are *jaloux* and *jalousie*, both of which derive from the Greek word *zelos*, which meant fervor, warmth, ardor, or intense desire. The French word *jalousie*, however, has a dual meaning. One meaning is similar to the English *jealous*, but *jalousie* also refers to a Venetian blind, the kind with numerous horizontal slats suspended one above the other. The Norwegian psychiatrist Nils Retterstol at the University of Oslo speculates that this meaning arose from a situation in which a husband suspicious of his wife could observe her undetected from behind the *jalousie*, presumably to catch her in the act of intercourse with another man. (p. 28, italics in the original)

The dictionary definition of jealousy includes phrases like "intolerance of rivalry or unfaithfulness ... hostility towards a rival or one believed to enjoy an advantage ... [and] zealous vigilance" (Mish, 1993, p. 627). Three realms seem to be involved here: emotional, cognitive, and behavioral. Close contact with someone afflicted with jealousy lends support to such categorization. In *the realm of emotions*, jealousy involves mental pain and mistrust. The former results from the subjectively experienced rupture of a self-object relation that was taken for granted (Akhtar, 2000; Freud, 1926d; Weiss, 1934). The latter is a reaction to the trauma of betrayal (actual or imaginary) and guards against recurrence of mental pain. In *the realm of cognition*, many disturbances are evident. The jealous individual sees meaning where there is no meaning, exaggerates the importance of environmental cues, and shows difficulty in considering alternate explanations for what he or she has deduced. A jealous wife, for instance, chides her husband who welcomes a couple entering their house for dinner by telling the female guest that she is looking "very nice"; the wife finds this an evidence of her husband's wanting to have sex with that woman. A jealous husband turns red with rage when, after giving a paper, his academician wife thanks her mentor before talking to him; he concludes that she does not love him at all. The jealous person's cognition is characterized by rigidity, loss of figure-ground relationship, and "narrow-mindedness" (Brenman, 1985) which has "the function of squeezing out humanity and preventing human understanding from modifying cruelty" (p. 273). In *the behavioural realm*, disturbing actions involve constantly looking for "clues" and "proofs" of betrayal, checking the lover's (or spouse's) email and text messages, and confirming their whereabouts (by repeatedly calling or actually showing up). Spying in other forms, stalking, and hiring private detectives also form the gamut of a jealous individual's behavior. Fortunately, in most instances, jealousy does not lead to such behaviors; it remains a private, if deeply troubling, experience. At other times, matters get out of hand and then not only the behaviors listed above come into operation but rage, violence, and even murder may take place.

Putting together the affective, cognitive, and behavioral manifestations of jealousy, it can be safely concluded that hostile mistrust, hypervigilance, and destructiveness constitute the central triad here. Blevis's (2009) monograph on jealousy contains all this and more. She notes that pervasive mistrust and the wish for omnipotent control are not the only features of jealousy. Among its other elements are (i) inability to understand that love cannot be controlled; (ii) perceptual errors (whereby a misspoken sentence, the slightest delay in responding to a phone call, a momentary shift in the eye gaze is imbued with paranoia and triggers panic); (iii) a split attitude towards the imaginary rival, who is consciously hated and devalued put preconsciously (or unconsciously) admired and envied; (iv) a profound sense of having lost the love that one was receiving, (v) a traumatic destabilization of identity; (vi) the activation of deep insecurity about one's "lovability"; (vii) insistent claims for attention and love; (viii) the potential of perverse sadomasochistic excitement in the experience of being "ignored" and "excluded," and finally (ix) a peculiar, thought-numbing alienation from the object of one's desire.

Even with this rich and nuanced portrait at hand, some questions about the nature of jealousy remain unanswered. These include the following.

- *Can a certain amount of jealousy be deemed "normal"?* From St Augustine's declaration that "He that is not jealous, is not in love" (cited in Buss, 2000, p. 27) to Freud's (1922b) allowing that ordinary "competitive jealousy" might be "normal," there exists a notion that a modicum of jealousy is inevitable in intimate relationships. Indeed, there is some evidence (Buss, 2000) that both women and men tend to regard a partner's absence of jealousy as lack of love.
- *What distinguishes normal jealousy from abnormal jealousy?* The sort of jealousy referred to above as normal is mild, fleeting, and correctible by reality testing. At times, a certain playfulness also characterizes the experience. Morbid jealousy, in contrast, is disturbing, persistent, and immune to corrective evidence from reality. Unlike normal jealousy which has the potential of fueling competitiveness with the rival and enhancing eroticism within the couple, pathological jealousy saddles the individual with chronic worry and becomes a torment for the partner.[1]
- *Are there "cocreated" elements in the experience of jealousy?* The impact of jealousy on one's lover or spouse is evident via the latter's feeling wrongfully accused, constantly watched, and treated unempathically. Such distress on the partner's part (and his or her defensive maneuvers of concealing one's whereabouts or restricting one's contacts) is customarily seen as a consequence of the jealous individual's tyranny. However, a deeper question exists here. Could the person predisposed to jealousy have "deliberately" picked a lover/spouse who possesses an extra quantum of jealousy-inducing triggers? For instance, an inwardly insecure man might marry a crowd-pleasing popular theatre actress, or a woman with shaky self-esteem might get involved with a recently divorced man with a four-year-old coquettish daughter in order to "facilitate" the subsequent development of jealousy. Such "actualization" (Akhtar, 2009a, p. 4) accords the jealous person's complaints a realistic quality. To a certain extent,

then, the couple's suffering is cocreated insofar as both partners are unable to free themselves from their characterological traps and both continue to hurt each other.

- *Can jealousy be "induced" or is the jealous person predisposed to such suffering?* Iago's cunning and relentless efforts to make Othello believe that his wife, Desdemona, is having an affair with Cassio (Shakespeare, 1603), would have us believe that jealous feelings can be induced by others. This might be true to a certain extent. There might exist environmental triggers that unleash the "green-eyed monster"; these include a partner's glance at an attractive stranger passing by, his undue friendliness with a good-looking waitress in a restaurant, or even his expression of love for his children from a previous marriage. However, such "induction" and "triggering" is generally more effective in people who already have a predisposition to jealousy.
- *Are there variables in one's personal background that predispose one to intense jealousy?* This question brings us to the psychoanalytic explanations of the origins of jealousy. Before covering that literature, however, going over a jargon-free and matter-of-fact passage from Ayala Pines's (1998) book, *Romantic Jealousy*, might serve us well. Pines states that the predisposition to jealousy:

> … is influenced by our family background: a man whose mother was unfaithful to his father or whose parents had violent out-bursts of jealousy is likely to have far greater predisposition to jealousy than a man whose father and mother felt secure in each other's love. It is influenced by our family constellation: a woman who was outshone by a prettier or brighter sister is likely to have a greater predisposition to jealousy than a woman who was the favorite child in the family. It is also influenced by childhood and adult attachment history: a person who had a secure attachment to his mother will be less likely to become jealous than an anxiously attached person, and a person who was betrayed by a trusted mate is likely to develop a greater predisposition to jealousy in the future. (pp. 6–7)

This descriptive portrait of vulnerability to jealousy is a good stepping-stone for us to enter into the chamber of metapsychology.

Psychoanalytic perspectives

Freud's views

Freud (1911c) first formulated the mechanism underlying jealousy in his study of the Schreber case. He directed his comments to alcoholic delusions of jealousy and delusions of jealousy in women. In both scenarios, he traced the origin of jealousy to latent homosexuality. An alcoholic was disappointed in his love for women and turned to men for company. His "drinking buddies," however, soon became "the objects of a strong libidinal cathexis in his unconscious" (p. 64). This, in turn, was transformed into jealousy by the following associational chain: "It is not *I* who love the man—*she* loves him" (p. 64, italics in the original). As a result, the man begins to suspect the women in relation to all the men who he himself is tempted to along similar lines: "It is not *I* who love the women—*he* loves them" (p. 64, italics in the original). The jealous woman suspects her male partner of paying excessive attention to all the women that she herself wants to be sexually involved with. Her dynamic was thus the exact replica of the male alcoholic. However, Freud added that the jealous woman is also attracted to women owing to "the dispositional effect of her excessive narcissism" (p. 64). Eleven years later, Freud (1922b) returned to the topic of jealousy and declared that:

> Jealousy is one of those affective states, like grief, that may be described as normal. If anyone appears to be without it, the inference is justified that it has undergone severe repression and consequently plays all the greater part in his unconscious mental life. (p. 223)

Freud felt jealousy was composed of three layers: (a) competitive, (b) projected, and (c) delusional. *Competitive jealousy* could be regarded as "normal." After all, the thought of losing one's love object does cause narcissistic injury and a tendency towards self-blame. Freud added though that:

> Although we may call it normal, this jealousy is by no means completely rational, that is, derived from the actual situation, proportionate to the circumstances, and under the complete control of the unconscious ego; for it is deep in the unconscious, it is a continuation of the earliest stirrings of the child's affective life, and

it originates in the Oedipus or brother–sister complex of the first sexual period. (p. 223)

The jealousy of the second layer, *projected jealousy*, is the result of the projection of *one's own* unfaithfulness (or the impulses towards it) upon the partner. The dynamic is the same in men and women. Those who cheat suspect others of cheating. Freud made the interesting observation that a certain latitude given to each partner's temptation to flirt with others serves as a safety valve and diminishes the need for repressing such impulses; this reduces the possibility of developing jealousy. *Delusional jealousy*, the third among Freud's nosology, also emanates from projection. However, the love object in this instance is of the same sex as the subject.

> Delusional jealousy is what is left of a homosexuality that has run its course, and it rightly takes its position among the classical forms of paranoia. As an attempt at defense against an unduly strong homosexual impulse, it may, in a man, be described in the formula: '*I* do not love him, *she* loves him'. (p. 225, italics in the original)

Freud quickly added that in most psychotic cases one finds an admixture of all three types of jealousy: competitive, projective, and delusional.

Freud's pupils and early followers

Ferenczi (1909) echoed Freud and, in reporting upon a female patient who was presumably also seen by the master, attributed the origin of jealousy to repudiated homosexual desire: "She projected it on to her husband (whom she had previously loved) and accused him of infidelity" (pp. 65–66). In a later paper, Ferenczi (1912) recounted the woeful tale of his own housekeeper. Her husband, a chronic alcoholic, repeatedly accused her of marital infidelity and of flirting with their master's male patients. Ferenczi offered all sorts of details about this alcoholic man's fascination with him and concluded that "The conspicuous feature of homosexual transference to myself allows of the interpretation that his jealousy of me signified only the projection of his own erotic pleasure in the male sex" (p. 161).

Jones too (1929) agreed with Freud that jealousy resulted from the projection of warded-off homosexuality. However, he arrived at this conclusion by a somewhat different and circuitous route. He held that the jealous person was possessed by narcissistic dependency. Such dependency had resulted from severe oedipal guilt which led to fear of the father and a desire for homosexual submission. This, in turn, led to fear of women from which infidelity arose; the projection of infidelity caused one to experience jealousy.

In contrast to such loyalty to Freud's formulations, Klein (1927) traced the origin of jealousy to the child's reaction to the arrival of a sibling. Noting that relationship with brothers and sisters plays a fundamental role in character formation,[2] Klein stated that:

> Every analysis proves that all children suffer great jealousy of younger sisters and brothers as well as of older ones. Even the quite small child, which seemingly knows nothing about birth, has a very distinct *unconscious* knowledge of the fact that children grow in the mother's womb. A great hate is directed against this child in the mother's womb for reasons of jealousy, and—as typical of the phantasies of a child during the mother's expectancy of another one—we find desires to mutilate the mother's womb and to deface the child in it by biting and cutting it. (p. 173, italics in the original)

Klein added that similar sadistic impulses are often directed against older siblings because the child feels weaker in comparison to them, even if this might not be the case in reality. Another important aspect of Klein's theorization involved the complex relationship between envy and jealousy. She distinguished envy as a dyadic and jealousy as a triadic experience. However, the way the two emotions were related becomes a little muddled in her writings. At one place, she spoke of infantile envy of the maternal breast and declared that "To this primary envy, jealousy is added when the Oedipus situation arises" (1952, p. 79). At another place, she reported that:

> There is a direct link between the envy experienced towards the mother's breast and the development of jealousy. Jealousy is based on the suspicion of and rivalry with the father, who is accused of having taken away the mother's breast and the mother. This rivalry marks the early stages of the direct and inverted Oedipus complex, which normally arises concurrently with the depressive position in the second quarter of the first year. (1957, p. 196)

At a third place, however, she states that the oedipal "envy, rivalry and jealousy—at this stage still powerfully stirred by oral-sadistic impulses—are now experienced towards two people who are both hated and loved" (1952, p. 80). This leaves the impression that oedipal jealousy was a revival, even if a powerful one, of oral sadism (directed at mother and siblings). Thus who was the child's original rival—a sibling or the father—remained unclear in Klein's writing. In all fairness to her though, it should be acknowledged that the inseparability of the two (after all, it is the father who impregnates the mother and causes siblings to be born) and her locating the oedipal development in the second year of life makes the separation of envy and jealousy rather murky. What does remain clear about Klein's formulation is that projection of homosexuality plays a little role and oral sadism (even though accentuated by the oedipal configuration) a big role in the genesis of jealousy.

Brunswick (1929), working with a female psychotic patient suffering from jealousy, found a compromise between the Freudian and the Kleinian positions. She agreed that homosexuality underlay jealousy but felt that such erotic inclination arose not from the Oedipus complex but from an earlier preoedipal level. Riviere (1932) gave this formulation a further twist. She felt that the desire to steal something from the mother or to rob her of her possessions was, in its projected form, the basis of jealousy. Riviere acknowledged that such robbing fantasies can undergo "genitalization" (i.e., acquire an adult sexual connotation) but are in fact infantile and oral in origin. She stated that in the jealous person

> … the "loss of love" or "search for love" in question refers ultimately to something deeper than a genital relation to the desired parent. The quality of the attachments in such people, moreover, is often that to a part-object, thus facilitating the change of real objects and explaining the relative indifference shown to their objective personality. The "search" or "loss" in such cases can be traced back to *oral envy*, and to the deprivation of the breast or father's penis (as an oral object)—the object with which the parents in coitus are at that level felt to be gratifying each other. I would mention here the very prevalent confusion between the *words* "envy" and "jealousy" which finds a quite precise derivation in this oral primal scene experience in which the two feelings would be indistinguishable. This and only this experience furnishes a rational basis for the acute

and desperate sense of lack and loss, of dire need, of emptiness and
desolation felt by the jealous one of a triangle and reversed by the
unfaithful. (pp. 420–421)

Fenichel (1945) too discerned early oral fixation at the base of jealousy.
Oral sadistic wishes directed toward the mother were projected on the
dyadic partner of adult life who, as a result, appeared treacherous and
cunning. Working independently in Calcutta and seemingly unaware
of Riviere's and Fenichel's contributions, Chatterji (1948) presented
detailed clinical material to support his conclusion that "Pathological
jealousy is not one of genital oedipal level but is of purely oral origin"
(p. 21). Barag (1949), reporting from Israel on a male case, however,
went back to the early Freudian formulation and did not evoke oral
fixation in the genesis of jealousy.

Later analysts

Siedenberg (1952a, 1952b) noted that a particular kind of wish-fulfilment
takes place in jealousy regardless of whether it is of day-to-day type or
of clinical severity. A modicum of feigned jealousy and gently teasing
"accusations" of flirtatiousness add spice to the romantic life of a well-
functioning couple. The husband who teases his wife about her fond-
ness of their gardener enjoys unconscious pleasure of oedipal victory
(with the gardener standing for the son and he himself for the father)
while in reality committing no transgression. The same goes for the wife
who jokes about her husband's "love" for his young research assistant.
In both instances, a certain lightheartedness is retained and the experience of jealousy is self-dosed and enjoyable.[3] When such playfulness is
lost, jealousy turns deeply distressing. However, even in such instances,
one can discern a wish-fulfilment to take place. By bitterly accusing the
partner of unfaithfulness, the individual betrays the desire that the parent who was the object of childhood erotic desire indeed be sexually
loose—so that one's illicit desires can be gratified on a clandestine basis.
Such covert wish-fulfilment in jealousy is responsible for the fact that
the jealous individual thwarts all reassurance and, contrary to all expectation, seeks "confirmation" of his or her suspicions.

Schmidberg (1953) emphasized the intense early need for the love
object, oral sadism, and desire for omnipotent control. She thus remained
loyally within the drive theory model and that too as it pertained to

the oral phase. In contrast, Ortega (1959) approached the problem of jealousy from a Sullivanian (i.e., interpersonal) perspective. He posited that jealous individuals are deeply insecure about their worthiness to others. As a result, their rivals need not be demonstrably superior; they are *felt* to be superior because one considers oneself worth nothing. Moreover, competing with them constitutes an effort to seem more adequate than the jealous person actually feels.

Writing a decade later, Pao (1969) questioned the inevitability of the link between repressed homosexuality and jealousy. He traced the origin of jealousy to disturbed object relations of early childhood. Pao stated:

> Because three persons act as the "stars" of the jealousy drama, it may be intimated that jealousy must be experienced at a time when the developing and maturing child acquires the ability to clearly distinguish persons around him. At such times, he must have already been able to distinguish self from others, to establish a certain degree of object constancy, and to formulate a rudimentary set of self-representations and object-representations. The intrusion on the dyadic relation between the mother and the child by a third person, such as the father, sibling, or others, is inevitable. Therefore, every child knows jealousy feelings as soon as his ego equipment permits him to conceptualize them. But, to formulate the self-representations and the object-representations in order to stage or re-stage the jealousy drama requires something special. (pp. 633–634)

This "special" thing was an actual event (e.g., birth of a sibling, separation from the mother) that created insecurity about attachment and belonging. The ensuing grief then got exacerbated by the feelings of exclusion during the oedipal phase. Pao went on to declare that jealousy is a complex mental state that involves all three components of the psychic structure: id (manifested by oral sadism), ego (manifested by projection of impulses to be unfaithful and by narcissistic self-holding), and superego (manifested by punishing criticism of the partner and also of the self). Pao's observation regarding the role of early trauma was "confirmed" by Spielman (1971) and Wisdom (1976); the latter described the jealous reactions of a twelve-month-old boy to the birth of a brother in striking details.[4]

Neubauer (1982) added a new twist to the phenomenology of jealousy by distinguishing it not only from envy but also from the infrequently invoked concept of rivalry. According to him:

> *Rivalry*, the striving for the exclusive access to the source (of needed supplies), implies an assertive, aggressive struggle against the rival ... Rivalry is an act, based upon the wish not to lose the object to the rival. Thus, in rivalry, the contact with the object is maintained. *Envy* is based either on the awareness of superior attributes of others or an idealization of these attributes. The libidinal component of this admiration is linked to resentment, self-devaluation, and sadness. *Jealousy* is the resentment of the love the third person receives or expects. It comes into operation when additional developmental factors are added to the rivalry, when gender identity is established, that is, when the phallic-oedipal organization has developed and when the triadic relationship has oedipal characteristics. (pp. 123–124, italics added)

Neubauer went on to state that rivalry can be mastered through competition or coexistence and jealousy by repossession of the object's love. Envy, however, poses greater difficulty since it involves aggression directed at the very object that is admired and loved. Neubauer's contribution was followed by two other significant papers on jealousy during the 1980s even though neither of them referred to his ideas. Coen (1987) offered a highly nuanced and multiply determined portrait of jealousy. In this view, jealousy is both a substitute for and a defense against full and deep intimacy with another person. It is a masturbatory equivalent which involves perverse scenarios of sexual relatedness.

> The cast of characters includes at least four roles: male and female sexual protagonists, an observer, and an audience witnessing the interaction between the three. The need for concrete evidence relates to denial, mistrust, and guilt, especially about feared destructiveness, as well as masochistic and narcissistic enhancement. The object choice in pathological jealousy involves a fantasied protector, and is basically homosexual, narcissistic. These defend against the dangers of passive needs of another person different from oneself, as well as of aggressive destruction. (p. 107)

Pierloot (1988) extended the jealous individual's tormented object relations to the realm of "impersonal objects." Noting that impersonal objects (e.g., fetishes, transitional objects) often stand for part-objects (in both a figurative and a literal sense), he elucidated the symbolic significance of Othello's handkerchief and Lady Windermere's fan (from the eponymous play by Oscar Wilde, 1893). Thus the pain of jealousy suffused not only one's relationship with human beings but also with the inanimate objects that linked one with those human beings.[5]

More recent contributors

One monograph (Mollon, 2002), an edited volume (Wurmser & Jarass, 2008), an interesting paper (Lewin, 2011), and Blevis's (2009) slim but impressive book constitute the more recent contributions on jealousy that merit our attention. Mollon's (2002) monograph, titled *Shame and Jealousy*, attempted to bring together the work of Melanie Klein and Heinz Kohut. It proposed that a disruption of early parental empathy leads to an evaluation of the self as lacking or inferior in some way. This, in turn, causes a vulnerability to shame and jealousy. The contributors to Wurmser and Jarass's (2008a) edited volume also stressed the role of shame in the genesis of jealousy. Their essential thesis was that jealousy arises from the inevitable experience in human relations of being "the excluded third" (in the primal scene, most clearly, but also while witnessing mother's attention to a sibling). They also noted the "advance" from jealousy to murderous vengefulness. Wurmser and Jarass (2007), in their own contribution to the book, maintained that "The sequence of *shame → envy and jealousy → revenge → feared retribution by even more archaic forms of humiliation* turns into a characteristic vicious cycle of repeated traumatisation" (pp. 173–174, italics in the original).

Lewin (2011) proposed the novel concept of "parallel identification" which worked as a shield against the painful experience of jealousy. Such identification was a sort of manic defense and functioned in the following way:

> The identifying subject merges with his object of desire through compulsive imitation. This merger holds the subject in a developmental cocoon of non-being that negates his perception of any rivals for the object's love. Parallel identification inhibits conscious

> jealousy, subsequently blocking the subject's capacity to evolve
> through empathy and fantasy. (p. 551)

Individuals using such a defense had arrived at the precipice of jealousy and withdrew from it by creating an impenetrable shield of self-sufficiency. There is a "make-pretend merger" (p. 568) with the love object underneath this shield which is held in place by uncrossable boundaries against two-person relatedness.

This brings our survey of psychoanalytic literature on jealousy full circle back to Blevis's (2009) book which I mentioned at the very outset of this discourse and to which I will refer again in the treatment section of this chapter.

Critique, synthesis, and further ideas

While holding some water (especially vis-a-vis the projection of one's own unfaithful impulses), Freud's vase of hypotheses had many holes. *First*, it is heavily tilted in favour of the vicissitudes of libido and takes little account of the role of aggression. *Second*, it places emphasis on the oedipal determinants of jealousy and overlooks that jealousy could arise from preoedipal conflicts as well. *Third*, it bypasses the contribution made by actual traumatic events during childhood (details below) to the vulnerability to jealousy. *Fourth*, it assumes homosexuality to be invariably ego-dystonic and in need of repression and projection. *Fifth*, it fails to account for jealousy in overtly homosexual men and women. *Sixth*, its separation of "alcoholic" and "female" categories is logically untenable. And *finally*, it shows a phallocentric bias in postulating narcissism as a basis for jealous insecurity in women and not in men.

Such weaknesses in Freud's conceptualization coupled with the overall shift in psychoanalysis from drive theory to object relations approach led to the emergence of alternate explanations regarding jealousy. At first these explanations accommodated Freud's emphasis upon latent homosexuality, even though they often did so in labored ways. Later on, this particular etiological dimension was totally dropped. Oral sadism, early disappointment in caretaking figures, and traumatic turning away of a major love object became the major causative explanations for jealousy. Complex fantasies, ego restrictions, and compromised superego functioning were added to the psychoanalytic description of jealousy as well.

Klein's distinction of envy as being dyadic and jealousy as being triadic was largely upheld by subsequent contributors. However, some further thought is needed about this demarcation. After all, there is a reason to covet an attribute (e.g., better looks, greater intelligence) that someone else possesses and that reason often turns out to be the belief that if one has that attribute then one would be more admired and loved by others (a third party). Envy thus contains a covert scenario of jealousy. Conversely, hatred for a rival receiving (in reality or imagination) a loved one's attention implicitly acknowledges admiration for the rival. Jealousy thus contains a covert scenario of envy. The two emotions, it seems, are always intermingled and can only be separated in their extreme forms. Their frequent interchangeability in colloquial discourse thus seems far from linguistic sloppiness; it actually contains a bit of wisdom. Mention of such colloquial wisdom brings us to consider the sociocultural aspects of jealousy.

Sociocultural aspects

The experience of jealousy is ubiquitous. With rare exceptions (e.g., the Banaro of New Guinea reported upon by the great anthropologist, Margaret Mead, 1931), all cultures show evidence of its existence. What differs from one culture to another is the act/event that triggers jealousy. Sexual liaison with someone other than the spouse, regarded to be the most powerful "justification" for developing acute jealousy, is not universally found to be so. In polygamous and polyandrous societies and among "swingers," sexual involvement with more than one partner is accepted as a norm (Gilmartin, 1986). Jealousy among the members of these groups is stirred up by emotional infidelity and social gossip. Moreover, cultures that uphold monogamous marriage as an ideal are more prone to stir up jealousy in general. Cultures that suppress women on a conscious basis (while idealizing and fearing them unconsciously) are more prone to cause male romantic jealousy in particular (Pines, 1998).

The link between idealization and jealousy becomes more evident when we discover that jealousy shares a feature with nostalgia. Both experiences have a bitter-sweet quality. The bitterness in them has to do with the loss of an idealized self-object state. The sweetness has to do with the memory of (in the case of jealousy) and the hope of reunion with (in the case of nostalgia) that idealized object. To be sure, nostalgia has more sweetness and jealousy more bitterness but both emotions contain the bittersweet flavor.

The bitterness of jealousy, if truly unbearable, can break hearts, rupture bonds, and lead to destructive acts. When manageable, the same bitterness can become fuel for sublimation. Vying to obtain similar, if not greater, acclaim than others accord to a rival can become a force for personality growth (Edward, 2011). Under fortunate circumstances, such jealous competitiveness can yield productive results. This is as true for athletics as it is for science. The Harvard-based geneticist, Richard Lewontin (1968), declares that science is a competitive and aggressive enterprise and "a contest of man against man that provides knowledge as a side product" (p. 2). Within hard sciences, the well-known rivalries between Robert Koch and Louis Pasteur, Thomas Edison and Nicola Tesla, and Humphry Davy and Michael Faraday have contributed much to theoretical advances and new discoveries. Within literature and art, the jealous competitiveness between Arthur Rimbaud and Paul Verlaine, William Wordsworth and Samuel Taylor Coleridge, and Ernest Hemingway and F. Scott Fitzgerald have also propelled artistic creativity. And, within our own field of psychoanalysis, the tensions between Freud and Ferenczi, Klein and Winnicott, and Kohut and Kernberg have enhanced theory and technique.

The relationship between jealousy and creativity is not exhausted here. Great works of literature have been devoted to this emotion. Almost all the great love epics of the world include reference to jealousy and its disastrous outcome. Shakespeare's *Othello* (1603) might be the best known of a focused literary work on jealousy but it is hardly the only one. Tolstoy's (1889) *The Kreutzer Sonata*, Hardy's (1891) *Tess of the D'Urbervilles*, and the much hated and much loved experimental novel, *Jealousy*, by Alain Robbe-Grillet (1957) recently made a list of ten top novels about jealousy prepared by the Man Booker Award winning British novelist, Howard Jacobson (cited in *The Guardian*, November 4, 2009). Fiction is not the only literary genre fascinated by jealousy, however. Poetry too bows its head at the poisonous altar of the emotion. Major and minor poets in all languages have penned songs, sonnets, and ballads about jealousy. One poem that stands out for its brevity, its psychological-mindedness, and its keen awareness of the sadomasochistic agenda of jealousy is William Strode's (1598–1645) "On Jealousy".

There is a thing that nothing is,
A foolish wanton, sober wise;
It hath noe wings, noe eyes, noe eares,
And yet it flies, it sees, it heares;
It lives by losse, it feeds on smart,
It joyes in woe, it liveth not;
Yet evermore this hungry elfe
Doth feed on nothing but itselfe. (1620, p. 51)

Strode's poem underscores the experience of loss, defensive vigilance, and masochism in jealousy. In contrast, Rupert Brooke's (1887–1915) poem, "Jealousy," emphasizes the envy of the rival and the sadistic impulses towards both the rival and the betraying beloved.

When I see you, who were so wise and cool,
Gazing with silly sickness on that fool
You've given your love to, your adoring hands
Touch his so intimately that each understands,
I know, most hidden things; and when I know
Your holiest dreams yield to the stupid bow
Of his red lips, and that the empty grace
Of those strong legs and arms, that rosy face,
Has beaten your heart to such a flame of love,
That you have given him every touch and move,
Wrinkle and secret of you, all your life,
—Oh! then I know I'm waiting, lover-wife,
For the great time when love is at a close,
And all its fruit's to watch the thickening nose
And sweaty neck and dulling face and eye,
That are yours, and you, most surely, till you die!
Day after day you'll sit with him and note
The greasier tie, the dingy wrinkling coat;
As prettiness turn to pomp, and strength to fat,
And love, love, love to habit!
And after that,
When all that's fine in man is at an end,
And you, that loved young life and clean, must tend
A foul sick fumbling dribbling body and old,

When his rare lips hang flabby and can't hold
Slobber, and you're enduring that worst thing,
Senility's queasy furtive move-making,
And searching those dear eyes for human meaning,
Propping the bald and helpless head, and cleaning
A scrap that life's flung by, and love's forgotten, —
Then you'll be tired; and passion dead and rotten;
And he'll be dirty, dirty!
O lithe and free
And lightfoot, that the poor heart cries to see,
That's how I'll see your man and you! —

But you
—Oh, when THAT time comes, you'll be dirty too! (1908, p. 45)

Jealousy also undergirds the central theme of many significant plays and movies, including Peter Shaffer's (1979) *Amadeus*—a stunning theatrical piece dealing with an admixture of envy and jealousy. Films such as *Laura* (1944), *Mildred Pierce* (1945), *Niagara* (1953), *East of Eden* (1955), *An Affair to Remember* (1957), *Suddenly Last Summer* (1959), *The Beguiled* (1971), and *Fatal Attraction* (1987) are some outstanding movies about jealousy.[6] Though not directly about this emotion, the Mike Nichols's evergreen *The Graduate* (1967) and Stanley Kubrick's *Eyes Wide Shut* (1999) also tackle the theme of romantic jealousy in powerful and evocative ways.

Such sublimated outcomes pertaining to jealousy must not make one overlook that at its core, the affect is corrosive of both the self and its relations to loved others. A nationwide survey of marital counsellors revealed that jealousy is a problem in one third of all couples seeking couples therapy (White & Devine, 1991). Jealousy can also lead to aggressive acts, violence, and murder. Spousal murder is often precipitated by intense feelings of jealousy (Chimbos, 1978; Mullen, 1996). Such dark outcomes of jealousy bring us back to clinical concerns and therapeutic management of jealous individuals.

Therapeutic considerations

A good beginning point here is constituted by Blevis's (2009) therapeutic approach to such patients.[7] Her way of working with them is anchored in the conviction that the one afflicted with jealousy is fighting a battle that is not contemporary but from his or her past. Bringing forth the muzzled voices and frozen sentiments related to the time when someone deeply important (e.g., mother, father) turned away from the child remains profoundly important. Blevis demonstrates a truly impressive skill in discovering such "buried treasures" of pain and linking them up with their contemporary interpersonal versions. The pathways she traverses to reach the past are varied and include a subtle enactment on the patient's part (p. 15), a telling dream (p. 27), seemingly inexplicable intrusions into the patient's free association (p. 39), and so on.

While reconstruction remains the mainstay of Blevis's approach, she is forever prepared to make transference interpretations, thus vivifying the past as it is lived out in the "here and now" of the clinical relationship. Moreover, she is keenly aware of the regressive pull exerted by the masochistic pleasure of jealousy and, in that realm, is willing to go beyond interpretation and reconstruction to strict limit-setting. Note the following comment of hers:

> I had to put our work online when Frank, almost to the point of rage, announced that he wanted to destroy all our recent hard-won insights and return to the jealousy he so enjoyed. If he wanted to follow that path, it would have to be without me. (p. 43)

Such limit-setting and "spoiling" of the sadomasochistic pleasures inherent in jealousy requires a brave tough-mindedness to accompany the characteristic soft-heartedness of the analyst. The analyst might have to go out on a limb and the patient might have to bear considerable suffering in such moments. Blevis acknowledges that "To unearth the past takes courage because it requires questioning situations that would be more comfortable to leave unexamined" (p. 16).

At times, the patient comes to this point and cannot bear the material that is getting "de-repressed" and/or becoming evident as a result of taking a new look at his formative years. The jealous woman, who built the "personal myth" (Kris, 1956) that her jealousy originated with her teenage discovery of a lurid extramarital affair of her father, and who now finds out that she had been painfully "dropped" much earlier by her mother (when her younger sister was born), cannot tolerate the latter discovery; it destabilizes her too much and makes her feel too angry with her mother whom she needs for all sorts of other reasons. The jealous husband, filled with rage at his vivacious (taken by him to be seductive) wife, who "accidentally" hears the family gossip that his younger sister might be the product of a secret liaison his mother had when he was five or six years old, is loathe the recognize the shadow of such a past upon his current marital transactions. Arriving at such junctures, some jealous patients drop out of treatment.

However, a one-person psychology explanation of this sort can also be self-serving on the analyst's part. Shifting the responsibility of the impasse or disruption to the patient can evade the analyst's contributions to the difficulty. Therapeutic inexperience, technical rigidity, empathic failure of a sustained variety, and specific countertransference blocks to careful listening can all contribute to failed treatments. To be sure, working with intensely jealous patients is not easy. The analyst has to be simultaneously involved in many tasks, some of which seem contradictory. For instance, the analyst must empathize with the pain of the patient (at the suspicion that her boyfriend is interested in another woman) without lending his imprimatur on the validity of her perceptions leading to that pain. Conversely, the analyst must resist the temptation to "educate" the patient about social norms. Statements such as "It is within proper etiquette to compliment a woman guest about her looks," or "Glancing over at a waitress does not mean your husband is inclined to be unfaithful to you," do not help. They only make the patient feel misunderstood. Even more risky is to include the words "jealousy" or "jealous" in one's interpretations. Such labels, tempting though they might be, are to be strenuously avoided. This is because the patient whose analyst refers to him or her as "jealous" or calls his or her feeling "a pang of jealousy" experiences such utterances as pathologizing and invalidating. Yet another difficulty arises from the pressure that the patient puts upon the therapist to "agree" that the partner's behavior was indeed improper. The "screen" functions of this demand also need to be interpreted. In other words, the patient's need for the analyst to "confirm" that a partner has been inattentive masks the necessity for the validation of an earlier betrayal by a parent.

As treatment unfolds, the analyst gradually realizes that the patient is making a contradictory demand upon him: to confirm the "badness" of the offending party and thus validate that the patient *is* being betrayed but at the same time to reassure that the patient is lovable and is being loved. From this eroticized threesome battle (the aggrieved patient, the desirable side of the partner, and the betraying side of the partner), the analyst can find his way to the underlying oedipal triangulation, at first, and then to a preoedipal split in the mother–child relationship. The analyst might then learn that both these configurations had found "credibility" in external fixating events of the patient's childhood (e.g., father's affair during his daughter's teenage years; mother's giving birth to a sibling when the patient was barely fourteen months old). A firm commitment to the "principle of multiple function" (Waelder, 1936) anchors the analyst's work ego under such circumstances. It also allows him to discern that in parallel to the externalized crises, subtle transferential re-creations of early traumatic scenarios are also taking place. These need to be interpreted as well and in fact, addressing them might render the analyst's interventions much greater credibility than merely extra-transference interpretation and/or reconstruction would afford.

An important prerequisite to conduct such work is a deep and ongoing contact with one's countertransference. The sadomasochistic tableau of jealousy is induced via projective identification into the analyst but this almost never takes a coarse or explicit form. A man jealous of his wife's attention to her brother might attempt to induce similar jealousy in the analyst; he might brag about the large sums of money he is donating to his cardiologist and make the analyst fee excluded and inferior. Attention to disguised derivations of such sorts is very helpful in formulating interpretations of transference of jealousy. All in all, a well-attuned oscillation between transference and current reality, between perception and affect, between reconstruction and interpretation, and between validation and deconstruction is what is needed in order to be helpful to jealous individuals.

Concluding remarks

In this chapter, I have delineated the emotional, cognitive, and behavioral components of jealousy. I have distinguished "normal" from pathological jealousy and, by surveying the extensive psychoanalytic literature on the topic, have traced the origins of the vulnerability to the latter. After a brief foray into the sociocultural realm, I have returned to the clinical realm and elucidated the pitfalls and challenges in treating individuals with intense jealousy. Now, as I arrive at the conclusion of this contribution, I note that three areas still need attention. These include: (i) evolutionary foundations of jealousy, (ii) gender differences in the experience of jealousy, and (iii) the complete absence of jealousy in some individuals. Brief comments upon each of these follow.

From the evolutionary perspective, jealousy is an adaptive or problem-solving device whose aim is to help us cope with a host of reproductive threats. Jealousy pushes us to ward off rivals with nonverbal threats, verbal injunctions, and aggressive behaviors. It communicates commitment to the partner and precludes his or her straying by heightened vigilance. To be sure, this motivational substrate of jealousy is not conscious. It is based upon "emotional wisdom passed down to us over millions of years by our successful forbearers" (Buss, 2000, p. 6).

The second matter that has remained unaddressed is the gender difference in the experience of jealousy. Evolutionary psychologists, psychoanalysts, and empirical researchers of human behavior concur that men and women experience jealousy differently and react to it in separate ways. This does not mean that members of either gender experience more or less jealousy than the other.[8] In fact, there is ample empirical research to demonstrate that men and women report virtually identical levels of jealousy (Buunk & Hupka, 1987; White & Mullen, 1989). They differ, however, in what they feel most jealous about and how they express their bitterness at the real or imagined exclusion. Both men and women are hurt by infidelity of their partners but men are far more distressed by their women's sexual infidelity and women by their men's emotional infidelity (Shackelford, Buss, & Bennett, 2002). Another difference has been observed by DeSteno and Salovey (1996). These researchers note that when a woman knows that her man is attracted to a particular feature in another woman and the woman drawing his attention has that feature, she feels jealous. Men, in contrast, feel jealous of men who excel in areas important to their own self-definition. In other words, women's jealousy is more object-related, men's more narcissistic. Finally, there is the issue of jealousy leading to violence. Here too, one finds differences in the two genders, with men being more likely to be driven by jealousy to commit violent acts and murder (Buss, 2000; Paul & Galloway, 1994; Pines, 1983, 1998).

The third and last area needing comment is the absence of jealousy in certain individuals. Freud (1922b), as noted earlier in this discourse, was skeptical in this context and regarded absence of jealousy as merely a conscious experience underneath which lurked the unconscious, repressed emotion. At the other extreme is the argument that if one has experienced a secure attachment in childhood, possesses robust self-esteem, trusts the partner, and carries no impulses to be unfaithful oneself, then one would be immune to jealousy. A realistic compromise between such skeptical and credulous viewpoints on the absence of jealousy is to regard the vulnerability to mild jealousy as ubiquitous and to regard excessive jealousy as pathological. In other words, those who claim to be never jealous likely have the morbid intensities of the affect in mind while making their pronouncements. But if nothing at all, including actual sexual infidelity of their partner, distresses them, then one has to question such "pathological tolerance" (Pinta, 1979) and the deficiency of healthy entitlement that leads to it. To paraphrase Nietzsche (1905), who said "A small revenge is humaner than no revenge at all" (p. 71), we can end this discourse by declaring that a bit of fleeting and correctible jealousy is more congenial to mental health than a complete absence of the emotion. If a dollop of playful eroticism gets added to such mild jealousy, matters are even better.

CHAPTER THREE

Lovelessness

Ibegin this chapter with a recent poem of mine (Akhtar, 2016, p. 17) about the delicious and mad passivity of falling in love. It is titled "Defenses":

> I want a giraffe with a goat's neck,
> and a dog that flies in air.
> I want a mountain of water,
> and a lake filled with steel.
> I want a soundless song,
> and a grave that whistles.
> A tree that walks
> and a train that goes nowhere.
> I want a four year old grandmother,
> and a twelve feet tall son.
> Only having all this can
> stop me from falling in love with you.

This poem is about the magic that pervades the air—due to the ego's joyous surrender to an idealized object (Freud, 1917e)—at the time of falling in love. The poem's surrealism is understandably manic.

Its perspectival transcendence is the result of a fusion between the ego and the ego ideal. Compare this excitement of love's beginning with the sober self-awareness and gratitude towards the beloved once love has become deeply ensconced in the heart; this is evident in the following poem of mine, titled "Through You" (Akhtar, 1985, p. 7).

> I have known love
> I have known what it is
> To be yielding while still in command
> To be demanding and yet be kind
> To be sensuous while remaining restrained
> To be inviting but only between the lines
> To be apart yet not distant
> To be close without getting intertwined
> To be concerned though not intrusive
> To be respectful but not in awe
> To be childlike but not childish
> To be generous without emptying the heart
> All this I have known through you
> Through you, my dear
> I have known love.

This poem celebrates the wisdom imparted by love. By recounting the ego-synthesis mobilized by the internalization of a loving object, the poem confirms that love serves as "a glue for the unified self-representation" (Settlage, 1992, p. 352). This poem's purview is the intrapsychic developments consequent upon the experience of being loved. It is about consequences.

The psychic distance between the first and second poem constitutes the journey of love. This is a terrain of majesty and mundanity, pleasure and pain, construction and deconstruction, and bondage and release. Love, to which the world's philosophers, poets, writers, and psychologists have devoted unerring and loyal attention, is the basic fuel for our existence, survival, and advance through the time we are allotted to live. It is therefore a great tragedy when human beings do not have love in their lives, either because they do not feel (or are not) loved by others or because they themselves do not love anyone.

To be sure, love exists in forms other than romantic love. These include love of parents and siblings, love of friends, love of pets, and love of aesthetics and collective causes. These loves are important and can, at times, prove to be of sufficient sustaining value for a given individual. More often, they fail to gratify man's deepest needs to belong and to be known in his or her veracity (Bion, 1963). From Freud's (1930a) viewpoint, such loves are aim-inhibited replicas of what was "originally fully sensual love, and it is so still in the man's unconscious" (p. 103). Hence such displaced gratifications cannot provide complete satisfaction of man's need for love. To this formulation, I would add that establishing (actually, reestablishing) a dyad with the hues of the infant-mother bond is an evolutionary and existential imperative that can only be fulfilled via romantic love.

It is therefore romantic love and its lack that form the topic of this contribution. I will begin it with a review of psychoanalytic writings on love. Then I will describe lovelessness of two varieties: that arising from ego deficits and that arising from intrapsychic conflicts. Following this, I will discuss the handling of such maladies in psychotherapy and psychoanalysis. I will conclude with some synthesizing remarks and by raising some further questions for us to consider.

Love

Freud's views

In a seminal statement that still forms a cornerstone of the psychoanalytic understanding of romantic love, Freud (1912d) noted "… two currents whose union is necessary to ensure a completely normal attitude in love … These two may be distinguished as the *affectionate* and *sensual* current" (p. 180, italics in the original). The affectionate current was ontogenetically the earlier one. It arose in connection with the early body and psychic care provided by the primary objects, especially the mother. The second, more specifically sexual current, arrived on the scene with puberty. It had to be synthesized with the affectionate current. Romantic love could then be expressed towards non-familial objects with whom a sexual union was permissible and possible. At times, however, the two currents could not be brought together and this resulted in a psychopathological state. The sphere of love in such people remained bifurcated into tenderness and sexual passion. "Where they love they do not desire and where they desire they cannot love" (Freud, 1912d, p. 183).

Freud went on to make distinctions in the erotic life of men and women. In men, there was a ubiquitous tendency for "overvaluation of the sexual object" (p. 181). Women, in contrast, continued to correlate sexuality with its earlier, childhood prohibition. To heighten sexual pleasure, therefore, men needed to debase their love objects (e.g., choose a woman who was socio-culturally inferior to them) and women needed to imagine (or actually create) transgressing a prohibition.

Two years after this contribution, Freud (1914c) addressed the topic of love from a different perspective. He now distinguished between narcissistic (arising from the ego's self-affirming needs) and anaclitic (arising from the ego's desire for the object's help-giving qualities) forms of love. He emphasized that the

> ... highest phase development of which object libido is capable is seen in the state of being in love, when the subject seems to give up his own personality in favour of an object cathexis ... A person who loves has, so to speak, forfeited a part of his narcissism, and it can only be replaced by his being loved ... Loving in itself, in so far as it involves longing and deprivation, lowers self-regard; whereas being loved, having one's love returned, and possessing the love object raises it once more. (pp. 76, 98–99)

Noting the interdependence of the two lovers, Freud hinted at the potential of mental pain inherent in romantic passion. He also noted the transcendent longing in love since each lover comes closer to his or her own ego ideal through unification with the beloved. In a subsequent paper, Freud (1915e) noted that a synthesis of libidinal and aggressive aims was also necessary for true, deep love. Still later, Freud (1921c) elaborated upon the sexual overvaluation of the love object and traced such idealization to the love object's

> ... being treated in the same way as our own ego, so that when we are in love, a considerable amount of narcissistic libido overflows onto the object ... We love it on account of the perfections which we have striven to reach for own ego, and which we should now like to procure in this roundabout way as a means of satisfying our narcissism ... *The object has been in place of the ego ideal.* (pp. 112–113, italics in the original)

Finally in 1930, Freud again addressed the "unusual state" of being in love, stating that at the peak of such experience "... the boundary between ego and object threatens to melt away" (1930a, p. 66). While acknowledging the exaltation that accompanies love, Freud once again emphasized the potential of pain in it: "We are never so defenceless as when we love" (p. 82). He went on to note that many individuals protect themselves against the pain emanating from the loss of the love object by directing their love not to one person but to mankind in general and its cultural institutions. Such "aim-inhibited affection" (p. 102) constitutes the basis of friendship and familial ties as well.

Views of subsequent psychoanalysts

Bergmann (1971) suggested that the bliss associated with falling in love involved a re-finding of a lost ego state, namely that experienced during early mother–child symbiosis.[1] Later (1980), he outlined five functions of the ego that are associated with this experience: (i) the ego has to realistically assess the qualities of the love object and evaluate the future of a relationship with it; (ii) the ego must integrate aspects of many childhood love objects into love objects of adult life; (iii) the ego has to counteract the superego so that the love object does not become incestuous in the mind even though some similarity with the primary objects will be inevitable, and even desirable; (iv) the ego must counteract the inner pressure on "re-finding the impossible, the replica of the longed-for symbiosis" (p. 69), and (v) the ego must avoid masochism in choosing a love object.

Bergmann emphasized that enduring love depends to a large extent upon "transmutation of the idealization into gratitude for the re-finding and for the healing of the earlier wounds" (1980, p. 74). He also declared that love's potential to give to the adult what he had never received as a child imparts to love a great restitutional quality. Ultimately, it is the harmonious coexistence of three elements that characterizes happy love relationships: (1) re-finding of early love object on many levels of development; (2) improvement on the old objects by receiving what one had not receiving during childhood, and (3) mirroring affirmation of the self.

The capacity to fall and remain in love also received attention from Kernberg (1974a, 1974b, 1995). In his view, two developmental achievements are necessary for this capacity:

> ... a first stage, when the early capacity for sensuous stimulation of erogenous zones (particularly oral and skin erotism) is integrated

with the later capacity for establishing a total object relation; and a second stage, when full genital enjoyment incorporates early body-surface erotism into the context of a total object relation, including complementary sexual identification. (1974a, p. 486)

The first stage is related to the integration of contradictory self- and object representations, attainment of object constancy, and the capacity for in-depth relations with others. The second stage corresponds to a successful resolution of the oedipal conflict. In a highly original state-ment, Kernberg (1995) pointed out a hitherto unrecognized aspect of being in love, stating that it:

> ... also represents a mourning process related to growing up and becoming independent, the experience of leaving behind the real objects of childhood. In this process of separation, there is also reconfirmation of the good relations with internalized objects of the past as the individual becomes confident of the capacity to give and receive love and sexual gratification simultaneously—with a growth promoting mutual reinforcement of both—in contrast to the conflict between love and sex in childhood. (1995, pp. 58–59)

Kernberg also emphasized that it is important that higher forms of ide-alization persist within the loving couple. Such idealization

> ... represents idealized identification, not with the body or even the person of the love object but with the values for which this per-son stands. Intellectual, aesthetic, cultural, and ethical values are included here; and I think this represents, in part, integration of the superego on a higher level, one linked to the new capacity for integrating tender and sexual feelings and to the definite overcom-ing of the oedipal conflict. At the same time, in this establishment of identifications with the love object involving value system, a move-ment from the interrelation of the couple to a relationship with their culture and background is achieved; and past, present, and future are thereby linked in a new way. (1974a, p. 210)

A deep commitment to each other and to the values and experiences of a sexual and intellectual life lived together prevents the couple's break-down during middle age. Under such circumstances, renunciation of newer erotic possibilities adds depth to the couple's emotional and sensual life.

In a series of contributions spanning over two decades, Kernberg (1995) addressed the barriers to falling and remaining in love (1974a), the nature of mature love (1974b), aggression and love in the relationship of a couple (1991b), the nature of erotic desire (1991a), and the role of superego functions in the life of a couple (1993). Kernberg also discussed the impact of gender on the experience of mature sexual love. Citing Braunschweig and Fain's (1971) theories, he noted that, for both the boy and girl, the early bodily care by the mother kindles the potential for sexual excitement. However, the mother's implicitly "teasing" erotic relationship to her boy remains a constant in male sexuality, whereas her subtle rejection of sexual excitement regarding her daughter inhibits the girl's awareness of her vaginal sexuality. As a result, men have greater difficulty in dealing with ambivalence toward women and need to synthesize the affectionate and the sexual imagos of women, whereas women are slower to integrate sexuality in the context of love. The way men and women handle discontinuities regarding love relations also differs:

> Women usually discontinue sexual relations with a man they no longer love and establish a radical discontinuity between an old love relationship and a new one. Men are usually able to maintain sexual relationship with a woman even if their emotional commitment has been invested elsewhere, that is, they have a greater capacity for tolerating discontinuity between emotional and erotic investment in a woman, in reality and in fantasy, over many years, even in the absence of a real ongoing relationship with her. (Kernberg, 1995, p. 84)

Altman (1977) noted that women have a greater sense of commitment in love relations than do men. He traced this relative contentment to an earlier event in the girl's development, namely, the shifting of her love from mother to father.

> This renunciation prepares her for renunciation in the future in a way the boy is unable to match. The steadfastness of commitment is, in this view, the renunciation of alternative possibilities, and the future woman has already made it in childhood. The boy has not, can not, and will not. (p. 48)

Benedek (1977) emphasized that the fundamental dynamic processes of love replicate those involved in a mother–child dyad. Through the repetition of mutually gratifying acts, each lover is internalized by his or her partner. Each becomes a part of the self-system of the other. The demarcation between narcissistic and anaclitic love also diminishes within a couple over time. Marriage is sustained by continuation of sexual love and presence of mutual respect. Its permanence depends on the ego-organization of the two partners and on their libidinal investment in the institution of marriage itself. Parenthood establishes a "biological link" (p. 75) between husband and wife and consolidates the psychological bond between them.

Chasseguet-Smirgel (1985) elucidated the picture of the ego ideal as it emerges within the context of mature love. She noted that four elements characterize this situation: (i) the nostalgic search for oneness with the primary object is not given up, but the ways of achieving it become different; (ii) the sexual satisfaction within the couple and their autonomous (and mutually supported) sublimations enhance secondary narcissism of the ego and diminish the ego-ego ideal gap; (iii) those aspects of internal and external reality that facilitate these sexual and narcissistic gratifications get positively cathected and the ego ideal is, to some extent, projected in the very means of access to such realities, and (iv) the pain over remnant longings for oneness with primary objects and incestuous gratifications is compensated for by the attachment to the love object and its sustained availability.

Finally, mention must be made of Krause's (2009) corrective to the commonplace psychoanalytic theory that skin eroticism without relationship with a "whole object" is by definition perverse. In Krause's opinion, however, such:

> ... body practices are not pathological per se, but are, in the majority of cases, highly sophisticated attempts to repair a defect in self via the body schema change, including the sexual partner as (partial) object .... As a rule, the more pre-genital perverse sexuality is possible instead of rage, given a severe narcissistic injury, the less destructive the scenario will be. The basic intention of this pre-genital perverse body practice is to keep the object alive. (p. 208)

Krause's reminder serves as an appropriate segue to approach the psycho-structural defects that often underlie the inability to love others.

However, before delving into that, it might be useful to summarize what has been presented so far and also to address certain inoptimally scrutinized aspects of love life.

Synthesis and further ideas

The psychoanalytic literature on romantic love emphasizes that an integration of libidinal and aggressive drives is essential for bearing the ambivalence that is inherent to all meaningful human relationships, including that of love. In addition, a merger of "affectionate" and "sensual" currents (Freud, 1912d) must take place in order for the lovers to be tender and considerate as well as erotically excited towards each other. Finally, renunciation of infantile omnipotence is needed for love to be grounded in the realm of possibility, and mastery of oedipal desire is required for love to be devoid of guilt.

In this portrait, what actually constituted the "affectionate" and "sensual" currents remained ill-defined until I filled the former gap and Kernberg the latter. I (Akhtar, 2009a, 2009b) deconstructed the "affectionate current" into six meta-capacities: (i) concern, (ii) curiosity, (iii) empathy, (iv) optimal distance, (v) forgiveness, and (vi) mutual playfulness. Kernberg (1991a, 1992) deconstructed the "sensual current" into (i) longing for pleasurable physical closeness with the loved one, (ii) identification with the sexual excitement of the partner, (iii) shedding shame and overcoming the partner's shame, (iv) desire for loss of all boundaries, (v) idealization of the beloved's body, (vi) teasing and being teased, and (vii) oscillation between the search for privacy and exclusivity on the one hand, and a radical shifting from sexual intimacy on the other.

While the need for the fusion of "affectionate" and "sensual" currents in mature romantic love is unquestionable, the centrality of sex to love and marriage remains open to further consideration. In my more recent book on immigration (Akhtar, 2011a), for instance, I have discussed how the linkages between love, sex, and marriage vary across cultures. In most Western societies of today, sexual intimacy, love, and marriage form the modal, expected, and acceptable sequence of events. In the gender-segregated societies of the Middle East and vast swaths of Asia, however, the sequence might be marriage, sexual intimacy, and love.[2] As a psychoanalyst, one must attempt to rise above ethnocentric biases and allow for diverse developmental trajectories and different timetables of drive-integration in individuals raised in "average-expectable environ-ments" (Hartmann, 1939) that are markedly different in nature.

Another area needing more thought is the step-by-step evolution, consolidation, and sustenance of a love relationship. Falling in love is, in Freud's (1930a), terms, an "unusual state" (p. 66); self-object boundaries get blurred and idealization prevails. Remaining in love becomes pos-sible only after the early excitement subsides and some disillusionment in the partner and in love's transformational capacity has been experi-enced and gracefully borne. Sharing a common value system, contin-ued sexual involvement, and an admiring attitude towards each other's sublimations helps the couple maintain love for each other. The gradual accruing of memories of shared experiences provides a new structure for the couple's emotional refueling. With age, each partner might lose parents, siblings, and friends to illness and death and both partners are compelled to let go of their children. The resulting psychic space has the potential of bringing the partners closer to each other than they ever have been before. The knife-sharp redness of a sinking sun then trans-forms itself into the cool white glow of a moon.

At the terminal end of this chronological progression an intriguing question arises. Is it possible that one can get satiated with love and fall out of love, not angrily or cynically but peacefully and with a sense of contentment? An ontogenetic prototype of this is the separation–individuation process of infancy and childhood (Mahler, Pine, & Bergman, 1975) and of adolescence (Blos, 1967). Both culminate in free-dom from primary objects. Could such "freedom" be a normative out-come of a very long-lasting love? And, if this is conceivable then turning to the realms of meditation, nature, and philosophy at that juncture might no longer be "aim-inhibited" gratifications but true loves of a special and autonomous variety. Let me hasten to add that the "falling out of love" of the sort I am speculating about here is, to my mind, a rare occurrence if it even exists. The falling out of love (and, inability to fall in love to begin with) one usually encounters in life is based upon psychopathology.

Lovelessness

The foregoing section has demonstrated that mature romantic love requires the achievement of many ego capacities. The most important among these are reality testing, fusion of libido, and aggression, and mastery of the Oedipus complex. A clear implication of this proposal is that in the absence of such ego capacities, the individual would not have mature love; he or she shall remain loveless, so to speak. This was made explicit by Balint (1948) quite early on in the psychoanalytic study of love. According to him, in order to love:

A. There should be no greediness, no insatiability, no wish to devour the object, to deny it any independent existence, etc., i.e. there should be no oral features;
B. There should be no wish to hurt, to humiliate, to boss, to dominate the object, etc., i.e. no sadistic features;
C. There should be no wish to defile the partner, to despise him (her) for his (her) sexual desires and pleasures, there should be no danger of being disgusted by the partner or being attracted only by some unpleasant features of him, etc., i.e. there should be no remnants of anal traits;
D. There should be no compulsion to boast about the possession of a penis, no fear of the partner's sexual organs, no fear for one's own sexual organs, no envy of the male or female genitalia, no feeling of being incomplete or of having a faulty sexual organ, or of the partner having a faulty one, etc., i.e. there should be no trace of the phallic phase or of the castration complex. (p. 43)

Balint acknowledged that no ideal case exists where these impediments have been completely overcome. Nonetheless, their continued existence, especially with a fierce intensity, can and does compromise the capacity to love. Balint's (1948) list is largely drive-oriented and follows the psychosexual scheme (oral, anal, phallic, oedipal) of "classical" psychoanalysis. Kernberg's (1974a) and Chasseguet-Smirgel's (1985) criteria (outlined in the previous section of this chapter) put a premium on ego capacities. The two perspectives are complementary and not contradictory. Drive-related fixations and ego-related deformations coexist in most clinically encountered cases of lovelessness. For didactic purposes though it might be useful to consider deficit-based and conflict-based forms of lovelessness separately.

Deficit-based lovelessness

In clinical practice and in life-at-large, one frequently comes across people who do not love anyone nor do they feel loved by anyone. They look sad and carry a deep streak of pessimism with them. Their eyes do not shine; instead there is either a sense of hollowness or pastiness to their glance. Such individuals have pronounced deficits in their capacities for concern, empathy, and basic trust. They cannot develop closeness with others. They lack spontaneity and manage their interpersonal lives on a factual basis. They also lack the capacity for "sexual overvaluation" (Freud, 1921c) and "idealization" (Bergmann, 1980; Kernberg, 1974a), which is mandatory as initial ingredient of falling in love. They are too "realistic" in their estimation of others and cannot allow themselves the perceptual compromise needed for idealization of another individual. An inward obliteration of gender markers, at times covered over by a patina of conventional gestures, also characterizes such individuals (Akhtar, 1992). Often they are celibate and given to masturbation with repetitive and banal fantasies. Even when they have somehow managed to enter into a marriage, they lack erotic desire and only go through the motions in their sexual life.

Dynamically, the inability of such individuals to fall in love emanates from a "lack of activation of early eroticism" (Kernberg, quoted in Akhtar, 1991a, p. 751) coupled with impaired basic trust and poor capacity for a sustained idealization of others. Attachment to others stirs up affects that are too intense for their deficit-riddled ego to manage. The developmental background of such individuals almost invariably reveals a history of severe, unmitigated childhood trauma. Physical and sexual abuse, parental desertion through divorce or death, and pronounced neglect of anaclitic and mirroring "ego needs" (Casement, 1991) from the earliest years of life form the background of this psychopathology.

Such individuals often have severely schizoid, paranoid, masochistic, and dis-affiliated antisocial personalities. They no longer search for love outside. They seem to have given up on finding a partner. They do not complain of lovelessness and have turned cynical with various rationalizations (e.g., age, finances). They equate their resigned stance with being "realistic." Deeper contact with such people, however, reveals that underneath their stoicism there does exist longing for love and, if not love, for passive nourishment and being taken care of. Fairbairn's (1952) and Guntrip's (1969) writings on the hidden yearnings of the schizoid individual come to mind in this context. In fact, long before them, Emile Kretschmer (1925), the great descriptive psychiatrist of Tubingen, had recognized that schizoid individuals were always sensitive, though the extent to which they overtly display this trait varied considerably. He emphasized that:

> ... even in that half of our material, which is primarily cold, and poor in affective response, as soon as we come into close personal contact with such schizoids, we find, very frequently, behind the affectless numbed exterior, in the innermost sanctuary, a tender personality-nucleus with the most vulnerable nervous sensitivity, which has withdrawn into itself and lies there contorted. (p. 153)

This sort of withdrawal is caused by chronic disappointments of love-seeking in childhood. Consequently, little faith is left to pursue love in adult life. Active loving is readily given up but feeling loved is no easy matter as well. In fact, it has its own psycho-structural prerequisites. According to Moore and Fine (1990), "Self constancy and sound secondary narcissism are necessary in order to feel loved" (p. 113). In fact, many other ego capacities need to be in place for this experience to occur, including the capacities to (i) experience humility and gratitude; (ii) recognize the value of the other, and hence tolerate envy toward him or her; (iii) renounce a cynical worldview and the masochistically tinged, deprived child representations of oneself associated with it, (iv) relinquish infantile omnipotence and be satisfied with inner and outer life being "good enough" and therefore, by implication, imperfect, (v) psychically surrender to attachment, hence feel vulnerable to separation and loss, and (vi) experience guilt, since some aggression towards the love object continues to emanate from within even under the best circumstances.

Many narcissistic, paranoid, and schizoid individuals lack these capacities and therefore cannot feel loved. In this context, the dark musings of Ben, the protagonist of Louis Begley's (1993) *The Man Who Was Late*, readily come to mind.

> Such as Veronique was, she made me happy as no one except Rachel. Before she began to press me to act like a normal man, she made me a good deal happier. The poor dummy actually loved me, Rachel knew better: her idea was that, for a time, I could love her on a live-in basis. Probably that is all I am good for, although for a while, with Veronique, I made progress—I was beginning to be able bear it without wincing, when she was nice to me. (pp. 221–222)

To extend a popular psychoanalytic metaphor, individuals such as Ben do not lack mirrors but have impaired visions! This prevents them from seeing their own libidinally invested reflections in others' affirming behaviors toward them. They *are* loved but do not *feel* loved.

Conflict-based lovelessness

Resembling the individuals in the former category, such persons are inwardly different. Their psychopathology does not arise from a deficit (i.e., not knowing *how* to love) but from conflict (i.e., not knowing *whether* to love). The sources of such conflict can be variable and range from those involving psychotic anxieties (Klein, 1927, 1930) to more symbolically structured and oedipally based neurotic anxieties (Freud, 1926d). At the former end are schizoid individuals who are terrified of giving themselves over to a relationship; they feel depleted after the slightest tender contact with others, especially if it demands that they bond with another person (Fairbairn, 1952). Yet, they are also afraid of never finding someone to love. They fluctuate between the poles of this "need-fear dilemma" (Burnham, Gladstone, & Gibson, 1969) in a characteristic "in and out programme" (Guntrip, 1969) of human relatedness. Often they give up loving altogether in order to avoid the dual terror of abandonment and engulfment. Yet another difficulty arises from the unconscious envy that gets stirred up toward the potential love object because, if loved, it appears to be receiving the libidinal supplies that the subject desires for himself (Klein, 1940). Not being able to fall in love under such circumstances acts as a defense against envy.

Individuals who turn away from love because of fear have often grown up with chronic neglect of their anaclitic needs as children. Like Ferenczi's (1929) "unwelcome child," they do not put much faith in others and in life's rejuvenating potential in general. Upon encountering loving and affirmative overtures by others, they act incredulously and regard those others as naïve and misled folk. Often this inability (or refusal) to accept the love that comes their way is associated with generalized anhedonia and lack of pleasure in any aspect of life. The more sophisticated among such individuals might be aware of their tragic, unloved childhoods and declare that they have permanent defects in their capacity to be loved; they say that having never been loved has robbed them of an experiential prototype of participating in a loving interaction. There may or may not be some truth to such claims but more likely is the fact that any glimpse of love stirs up in them greed and the consequent terror of being dropped and abandoned all over again. Their fear mobilizes their rejection of love.

Less severe psychopathology can also contribute to inhibitions of loving. Pronounced oedipal fixation, arising from marked primal scene exposure and perversely stimulating anal intrusions during toilet training can result in a tenacious obsessional character organization. Capacities for tenderness, concern, optimal distance, and erotic excitement get regressively contaminated by startling amounts of castration anxiety and by sexual life readily getting translated into the language of an "anal universe" (Chasseguet-Smirgel, 1984), that is, a psychic cosmos of "purity," pseudo-aesthetics, and denial of genital differences. As a result, active loving stirs up deep superego anxiety at a higher level and loss of contact with a differentiated other on the lower level. The defense then is to stop loving altogether and lead a mathematically governed life of rituals and routines.

Synthesis and further ideas

The preceding descriptions of deficit-based and conflict-based forms of lovelessness have left little doubt that such categories are valid only for the extremes of this malady. More often than not the psychopathology is a hybrid of deficit and conflict. The same applies to the active and passive dimensions in this realm. Not being able to love and not feeling loved also coexist on a frequent basis. To be sure, one aspect of the problem might be more overt than the other in a given instance but the latter also comes to the surface sooner or later. In a "mirror complementarity of the self" (Bach, 1977), the unloving self hides the unloved self, or vice versa.

Another development worth noting is that the mind finds substitute gratification in the absence of love. Proud self-reliance, especially when imbued with "moral narcissism" (Green, 1986) constitutes one such source of pleasure. A more bleak situation is presented by individuals who are inwardly tied to a "dead mother" (Green, 1980), that is, the introject of a mother who was devoid of all concern, affection, solace, and psychic nourishment towards her child. Individuals with this malady can find no love for themselves from within. And, by externalizing such an unforgiving inner presence, fail to find love in the outside world as well. Theirs is a tormented existence of empty (i.e., lacking fantasy) masochism.

They are blind to the loving gestures of contemporary figures and cannot unshackle themselves from the bondage of loyalty to their inner "dead mother." Any movement away from this submission frightens them for, deep down, they continue to hope that "somebody …" (Akhtar, 1996) the "dead" mother might come alive and they might resume life from its earliest steps all over again.

In contrast to such persons are the individuals who suffer from the "syndrome of malignant narcissism" (Kernberg, 1984) which shows the coexistence of (i) a typical narcissistic personality disorder, (ii) antisocial behaviour, (iii) ego-syntonic sadism, and (iv) a deeply paranoid orientation towards life. Individuals with this syndrome idealize their destructive potential and their callous solipsism (Rosenfeld, 1971). They seek to defile and destroy whatever love is offered to them in order to maintain a cold and contemptuous superiority over others. They mock tenderness and glorify hatred. In becoming totally identified with the omnipotent destructive aspect of their selves and their internalized "bad" objects, they kill off their sane and loving self-representations, which "threaten" to develop attachment and dependence. The less disturbed among this group are wistfully aware of their inner imprisonment but feel that there is little anybody (or they themselves) can do to unhinge this Faustian bondage. The following admission by a character in Allen Wheelis's (1994) *The Way Things Are*, eloquently captures this dilemma.

> I don't allow for the fuzziness, the inexactness of life, that will never conform precisely to any pattern. I rule out error and laughter and slippage, and so take away hope for betterment, for decency. I pull them down into despair. My despair! That's it! If I can't make them love me. But they do! Clara loves me! What is it then? If I cannot make them find some way to relieve my fear so that I can accept love—that's it!—then I will drag them down into my vision of absolute, inescapable evil. How despicable I am! (p. 125)

Such sadomasochistic proclivity can get glorified in the mind of its possessors. Consequently, they "choose" to lead a life of mistrust, isolation, and contempt for attachment. At other times, narcissism fails to bind the aggression inherent in such attitudes. More overt suffering then ensues. Visiting internet dating sites, hanging out alone in bars, and yearning for serendipitous encounters sustains a modicum of hope but in the private corners of the self, one knows that one is lost and needs help.

Implications for treatment

The foregoing delineation of various types of unloved and unloving patients had set the ground for attuned listening in the clinical situation. Such psychodynamic and psycho-structural differential diagnosis helps the clinician in empathizing with his patients' difficulties, to discern the obstacles in his way to loving and being loved, and to interpret with greater accuracy and effect. Three caveats, however, need to be entered here.

- *First*, feeling unloved and unloving often coexist. The clinician must therefore remain mindful of complexity and hybridity of phenomena in this realm and avoid premature closure of hypotheses.
- *Second*, it should be remembered that deprivation of love in childhood does not leave a hole in the child's psyche that can be filled by love given during adult life. The situation is not like acute deficiency of this or that nutriment that can be corrected by replenishing supplies. It is rather like a chronic insult to a system that develops malformed pathways and structures as a result. Love deprivation in childhood leads to a cauliflower of affects and fantasies: mental pain, hate, revenge fantasies, greed, self-doubt, lack of healthy entitlement, masochistic clinging to the internalized bad objects, and so on. Love offered in adult life fails to bypass this complex of emotions, it just does not help. Gradual interpretive resolution, both within and outside of the transference, is inevitably needed.
- *Third*, in a measure that seems to go against what has just been said, the patient must be allowed "for a sufficient length of time and at different levels to experience the soundness of the therapeutic rapport and the security of being understood" (Amati-Mehler & Argentieri, 1989, p. 303). The analyst must exercise patience to a far greater degree and for a much longer time than usual. The analytic process "must not be hurried by interpretations, however correct, since they may be felt as undue interference, as an attempt at devaluing the justification of their complaint and thus, instead of speeding up, they will slow down the therapeutic process" (Balint, 1968, p. 182).

What becomes eminently clear from the foregoing passages is that an optimal and individually tailored mixture of holding and interpretive interventions is necessary for treating patients who either do not feel loved or do not possess the capacity of love. The analyst needs to have the right techniques and, perhaps more important, the right attitude, it seems. The mention of right attitude brings up the thorny question of the analyst's love for the patient. Does such a thing actually exist? What sort of love is this? Can it be expressed? How? What are the potential risks and benefits of its expression? Can only "non-erotic" love be expressed or it conceivable that the analyst's revealing of erotic feelings towards the patient can be therapeutically beneficial? Questions abound in this realm and literature seeking their answer has grown considerably since the beginning days of psychoanalysis and especially over the last few decades. A brief survey follows.

While Freud has spoken of the "healing power of love" (1907a, p. 22) in a literary context and acknowledged that "our cures are cures of love" (1907a, cited in Nunberg and Federn, 1962, p. 101), in the papers on technique he opted to emphasize "neutrality" (1914c) and "abstinence" (1915a). He even went on to say that the analyst must avoid giving the patient "out of the fullness of his heart … all that a human being may hope to receive from another" (1919j, p. 163). His use of "surgeon" and "mirror" metaphors (1912e, pp. 115 and 118 respectively) furthered the ideal of an emotionless analyst who offered little apart from interpretation to his patient. That Freud himself broke such "rules" frequently and behaved in much more humane ways with his patients somehow did not permeate his "official" stance on therapeutic technique.

Disagreements soon surfaced, though. Freud's early pupil, Sandor Ferenczi, who was both culturally and characterologically distinct from Freud,[3] began to emphasize the importance of experiencing total acceptance at the heart of the therapeutic action in contrast to the exclusive role of insight resulting from interpretation (Ferenczi, 1911, 1928, 1930, 1931). He tried to reactivate the traumas of childhood in treatment in order to find a new resolution by offering what had previously not been available: a trusting and loving atmosphere (see Haynal, 2002, for a thorough explication of this). Continuing in a similar vein, Ferenczi's analysand, Michael Balint (1953) published a monograph titled *Primary Love and Psychoanalytic Technique*. Balint emphasized that early phases of personality development did not revolve around the epigenetic unfolding of instincts (e.g., oral, anal, phallic) but centered upon a search for love.

He stated that "The original and everlasting aim of all object relations is the primitive wish: I must be loved without any obligations on me and without any expectation of return from me" (p. 247). When this childhood need was not met, narcissism and aggression took the center stage of psyche. Treatment technique thus depended upon the analyst bearing these regressive phenomena, offering love and acceptance, and making it possible for the patient to experience a "new beginning."

Ever since Ferenczi's and Balint's departures from the restrictive "abstinence" of the early Freudian technique, a schism has existed—in fact, deepened—in the perspective on the analyst's role in the course of treatment. While the proponents of the "classical" approach (e.g., Brenner, 1955, 1976; Busch, 2004; Gray, 1994) continue to focus upon the painstaking and step-by-step interpretive process, those in favour of the sort of "leniency" advocated by Ferenczi and Balint see things differently. Greenson (1958) and Stone (1961) added the prefixes "passionate" and "benevolent" to the term "neutrality." Racker (1968) insisted that the analyst needs to have a parental sort of love for his patient to properly conduct analysis. Loewald (1960, 1970) believed that the intense study of truth (that each analysis is) requires genuine love; he felt that the analyst must have an encouraging and affirmative vision of his patient's potential. Schafer (1983) talked of the "appreciative attitude" of the well-functioning analyst towards his analysand. Fox (1998) used the term "unobjectionable positive countertransference" for professionally appropriate and personally ego-syntonic affectionate feelings of the analysts towards their patients. Many other such concepts have been proposed since then (see L. Friedman, 2005, for an impressive review and critique of this literature).

Cooper (1988) highlighted this tension between the abstinent and affectionate poles of analytic technique by comparing the seminal contributions of Strachey (1934) and Loewald (1960) to our understanding of the therapeutic action of psychoanalysis. More recently, writing in a special issue of *Psychoanalytic Inquiry* on analytic love, Ellman (2007) delineated the dialectical relationship between analytic love and transference resolution. He felt that one reinforced the other.

> Gradually, as love develops between the analytic pair, the ruptures that occur in the transference cycles are more easily endured. As love develops, the survival of the analytic pair is less and less of an issue. In addition, the necessary ruptures that occur in transitions

between the transference cycles are also more easily endured. Surviving each rupture enhances analytic trust and deepens the love between the analytic pair. (p. 246)

A similar sentiment was voiced more explicitly by Gerrard (2011) who declared that:

Until and unless there can be felt moments of love for the patient by the therapist, the patient is not able to develop fully. I think it is only when a patient can arouse our deepest loving feelings (not empathy) that we can really hope for a truly positive outcome with our work. (p. 51)

While Gerrard and Ellman do not actually define the sort of "love" they are talking about, other aspects of their contributions suggest that such love is one of parental (especially maternal) care and tenderness. And, this is true of almost all other contributions to this topic. Celenza (2014) is an exception in this regard since she speaks of the most tabooed love of the analyst, namely his or her erotic countertransference towards the patient. Addressing the thorny question of erotic countertransference revelations, she suggests abiding by the following guidelines: (i) the patient must have already surmised that the analyst returns his/her erotic feelings; (ii) the patient must have become increasingly able to detect his or her impact upon others and therefore be in lesser need of verbal confirmations from them; (iii) the analyst's disclosure must remain an "as-if" quality and "hold the line between the concrete and the symbolic" (p. 73); (iv) the interchange can underscore mutuality in the analytic experience but must not sacrifice asymmetry that is inherent in analytic work; (v) the disclosure of erotic countertransference must not be done to overcome a therapeutic impasse, and (vi) this intervention must be discussed with a supervisor, a colleague, a consultant, or a peer group.

However, erotic countertransference of proportions that need serious attention only develops with patients who are seductive, eroticized, and "loving" to a greater or lesser extent. The sort of patients who constitute the main concern of this chapter are loveless and unloving. They do not evoke such a countertransference reaction. And, this brings up the final issue and it is that the very patients who fail to evoke our love (due to their masochistic needs, sadistic attacks upon the analyst, or narcissistic self-absorption) are the ones most in the need of our love. At this point, we find ourselves coming full circle back to Ferenczi (1929) who stated that a patient who grew up with chronic and severe deprivation in his childhood:

> … had to be allowed for a time to have his way like a child, not unlike the "pre-treatment" which Anna Freud considers necessary in the case of real children. Through this indulgence, the patient is permitted, properly speaking for the first time, to enjoy the irresponsibility of childhood, which is equivalent to the introduction of *positive* life impulses and motives for his subsequent existence. Only later can one proceed cautiously to those demands for privation which characterize our analyses generally. (p. 106)

Concluding remarks

In this chapter, I have discussed the important topic of love and what its absence does to the human mind. I have surveyed the psychoanalytic writings on romantic love and described the maladies of not feeling loved by anyone in the world, and of not loving anyone in the world. A step-by-step deconstruction of the intricate psychodynamics of these conditions has led me to consider the technical strategies in dealing with them in the course of psychoanalysis and psychotherapy. While these are not my main areas of concern, I have also paid attention to the variables of age, gender, and culture-at-large.

Allow me now to conclude by reemphasizing the powerful role love plays in safeguarding, sustaining, and enriching our lives. It is love that makes us bear frustrations without despair. It is love that helps us overlook blemishes in others (and, in our own selves). It is love that propels our epistemic instinct, our concern for coming generations and this planet (Erikson, 1950). It is love that facilitates letting go of what can never be and living in a less-than-omnipotent manner. It is love that bestows upon us the grace of tenderness towards children, the elderly, the infirm, trees, rivers, and the little and big animals around us. It is love that makes us good students, artists, physicians, and poets. Lack (or, total absence) of love is always deleterious to the human mind. We might survive and even succeed on an external basis but the heart thus broken weeps inconsolably at night. To be sure, some stoic souls can turn lovelessness into a virtue; a character in Harold Pinter's (1975)

No Man's Land, for instance, proudly declares, "I have never been loved. From this I derive my strength" (p. 30). Such dark valor is an exception though. More often feeling unloved and feeling incapable of loving results in hapless anguish and chronic despair. One feels out of this world, an alien. There is no one to belong to and no one belongs to oneself. Emotionally untethered, the self begins to dim and lose meaning. The hustle and bustle of the day might keep one distracted but nights are hard. Not finding a good object, one is left to encounter the internal bad objects with poisoned monotony. This very scenario is depicted in the following poem of mine, "Blue" (Akhtar, 2014b, p. 16).

> The suitcase of unrealized dreams
> Sits heavily on the floor of a ravaged heart.
> Yearning opens its mouth.
> Loneliness dances in air,
> A demonic grin on its face.
> Tonight, the battle will be bloody, indeed.

PART II

SORROW FELT TO BE EMANATING FROM INSIDE

CHAPTER FOUR

Shamelessness

Sixteen years ago, as I was writing a review of Joseph and Ann-Marie Sandler's (1998) book, *Internal Objects Revisited*, Joseph Sandler died and my essay took on the flavour of an obituary. I felt compelled to go beyond the confines of a book review and to survey the milestones of this distinguished psychoanalyst's career. I began this portion of my writing with the following sentence: "Joseph Sandler's contributions to psychoanalysis are wide-ranging and, with shameless brevity, can be summarized under four categories" (Akhtar, 1999a, p. 533). Curiously, the phrase "shameless brevity" became a source of literary pride for me over time. But was I being really shameless? Or, was the ironic *mea culpa* a lexical veil to cover up the shame over what, of necessity, was a cursory treatment of someone's profound and vast oeuvre? In other words, was seeming shamelessness hiding shame? And, what is shamelessness anyway?

The fact is that we know little about it. While psychoanalytic literature on shame has grown in leaps and bounds over the years (Grinker, 1955; Kilborne, 2005; Lansky, 1991, 1994, 2003a, 2003b, 2007; S. Levin, 1967; Morrison, 1989; Spero, 1984; Wurmser, 1981), shamelessness finds little mention in this literature except in Wurmser's (1981) book on shame.

There is no entry on "shamelessness" in the major dictionaries of psychoanalysis (Akhtar, 2009a; Auchincloss & Samberg, 2012; Eidelberg, 1968; Laplanche & Pontalis, 1973; Moore & Fine, 1968, 1990) or in the indices of the *Standard Edition* or monographs on shame (e.g., Morrison, 1989). And, PEP Web—the electronic compilation of psychoanalytic journal articles spanning over a century—contains just one paper with the word "shamelessness" in its title (Lowenfeld, 1976). This paper is essentially a culturally inclined lament about the "spread of general shamelessness" (p. 69) in modern society and deems such decline of shame to be a threat to civilized living. The paper does not deconstruct shamelessness along descriptive, developmental, or metapsychological lines and leaves us titillated but unfulfilled.

I intend to fill this lacuna in the psychoanalytic knowledge in this realm. I will delineate the phenomenon of shamelessness, describe its various forms, and the sociocultural slant that can be readily given to its perception and even its existence. I will also make a few comments about the technical implications of the concept of shamelessness and conclude with some summarizing reflections. Before undertaking this sojourn, though, it might seem advisable to reiterate briefly our psychoanalytic understanding of shame.

Shame

Freud's views

Sigmund Freud included shame among the "repressing forces" (1895, p. 221) acting against the sexual instinct. He proposed that hysterical conversion symptoms were attempts to avoid reexperiencing the shame associated with childhood sexual seduction. Shame, in such signal form, was a motivator of defense in neurosis. In perversion, however, the sexual instinct could go to "astonishing lengths" (1905d, p. 161) to override the barrier of shame. Besides this difference in the dynamic role of shame in these two pathologies, Freud (1897, 1905d) distinguished between the ontogenesis and severity of shame across genders. He asserted that the development of shame occurs in "little girls earlier and in the face of less resistance than in boys" (1905d, p. 219); as a result, the tendency towards repression of sexuality is greater in the former. This difference becomes more prominent during puberty when girls are seized by sexual repugnance and boys by sexual desire.

For at that period a further sexual zone is (wholly or in part) extinguished in females which persists in males. I am thinking of the male genital zone, the region of clitoris, in which during childhood sensitivity is shown to be concentrated in girls as well as in boys. Hence the flood of shame which overwhelms the female at that period, till the new, vaginal zone is awakened, whether spontaneously or by reflex action. (1897, p. 270)

Freud (1908b) also noted that shame functions as a powerful force to cause repression (and, later, reaction formation) of anal erotic impulses. Later, he observed that "It is very remarkable that the reaction of shame should be so intimately connected with involuntary emptying of the bladder (whether in the daytime or at night) and not equally so, as one would have expected, with incontinence of the bowels" (1918b, p. 92). Freud speculated that such reactions represent precipitates from the history of human civilization, an idea that he reiterated in *Civilization and Its Discontents* (1930a). There, he speculated that: "Man's raising himself from the ground, of his assumption of an upright gait, made his genitals, which were previously concealed, visible and in need of protection, and so provoked a feeling of shame in him" (p. 99). In a later, full paper on the relationship between urination and shame, Freud (1932a) related man's domestication of fire to his controlling the desire to urinate on it and put it out; the loss of bladder control thus came to be looked down upon in man's history and became a source of shame.

Yet another realm in which Freud (1897, 1900a) talked of shame was that of dreams. He spoke of the common dream of being totally naked or inoptimally dressed in public with profound feelings of anxiety and shame. Curiously, the people around one in the dream do not seem to notice this state of undress. Freud attributed such dreams to the childhood experience of exhibiting oneself where the parental "horror" (actual or playful) is reversed by the process of wishful fulfilment.

Freud (1908e) also laid down the groundwork for distinguishing between shame and guilt when he wrote: "The adult is ashamed of his phantasies and hides them from other people. He cherishes his phantasies as his most intimate possessions, and as a rule he would rather confess his misdeeds than tell anyone his phantasies" (p. 145). Finally, Freud (1914c) noted that feelings of inferiority (from which shame arises) develop from the failure to live up to the narcissistic aspirations of the ego ideal.

Subsequent contributions

Fenichel (1945) discussed shame at length and concluded that it is deeply connected to urethral eroticism. Echoing Freud (1918b), he noted that while fecal incontinence in children receives direct punishment, deliberate and/or unintentional urinary incontinence (including somnolent bed-wetting) is often responded to by parental induction of shame. Internalization of this parental reaction causes vulnerability to shame, especially when urethral pleasure (and its derivatives) is in ascendance. Fenichel also noted that shame can serve as a defense against exhibitionism, and the syndrome of "social anxiety," with its chronic dread of rejection and being shamed, exists midway between the child's fear of castration or loss of love and the adult's bad conscience.

Erikson (1950) included "shame and doubt" in the polarity faced by the child during his or her third year of life; the other end was constituted by a sense of "autonomy." Lack of self-control and over-control by parents lead to a lasting propensity for shame; this affect emerges from feeling exposed and conscious of being looked at. "Doubt is the brother of shame" (p. 253), declared Erikson, adding that doubt has to do with continuing uncertainty about who (the parent or the child) is in charge of the child's sphincteric control and his sense of agency in general.

Piers and Singer (1953) located the origin of shame in the tension between ego and ego ideal. Shame, according to them, arises when a desired goal is not reached or one fails to live up to one's cherished self-image. Interestingly, Piers and Singer regard failing in one's own eyes as far more related to the feared and negative assessment by siblings and peers than by parents (and, of course, their respective introjects).

Kohut's views on shame were intricately related to his emphasis upon the self. Early on, when his concepts were ensconced in the structural model of the mind, Kohut (1966) proposed that shame results from the failure of the ego to "provide a proper discharge for the exhibitionistic demands of the narcissistic self" (p. 441). Ego ideal, in this formulation, attempts to keep exhibitionism to a minimum and thus becomes an ally of the superego. Later, Kohut (1971) changed his formulation and suggested that shame "is due to a flooding of the ego with un-neutralized exhibitionism[1] and not due to a relative ego-weakness vis-à-vis an overly strong system of ideals" (p. 181). Still later, Kohut (1972) traced the eruption of "narcissistic rage" to the experience of humiliation and shame. He also held that when, during middle age, an individual realizes that he or she has not lived up—or even come close—to his or her dreams, profound sadness and shame set in. Kohut (1977) spoke of a time:

> … of utter hopelessness for some, of utter lethargy, of that depression without guilt and self-directed aggression, which overtake those who feel that they have failed and cannot remedy the failure in the time and with the energies still left at their disposal. The suicides of this period are not the expression of a punitive superego, but a remedial act—the wish to wipe out the unbearable sense of mortification and *nameless shame* imposed by the ultimate recognition of a failure of an all-encompassing magnitude. (p. 241, italics added)

Picking up the theoretical discourse where Piers and Singer (1953) had left off, Chasseguet-Smirgel (1985) delineated the following sequence:

> The wish to receive narcissistic confirmation from one's peers to diminish the margin between the ego and the ideal leads the subject to exhibit himself to them. If this exhibition fails to ensure such satisfaction (i.e., if a narcissistic injury or "social humiliation" results) … the narcissistic injury [becomes] equivalent to a castration, and the exhibition to the exposure of the anus. This "about turn" (literally of a narcissistically cathected phallus) may be compared to the discovery of the fecal phallus beneath the gilt that seeks to mask it. (p. 161)

Chasseguet-Smirgel went on to add that the affect of shame can be disastrously painful and lead to suicide.

> This would then represent a realization of the phantasy that accompanies this affect: that of disappearing, of no longer having to meet the eyes of one's peers. The person who is ashamed is said to be unable to look others in the face, to be unable to face up to them, the hidden anus now being written on his face. One "dies of shame"; and to claim that ridicule cannot kill is but a denial. (p. 203)

Mention must also be made of the two important monographs on the topic of shame that appeared during the 1980s. These were *The Mask of*

Shame by Leon Wurmser (1981), and *Shame: The Underside of Narcissism* by Andrew Morrison (1989). While it is not possible to summarize their entire contents here, it is important to list their major points of emphasis. Wurmser regarded shame to be a polymorphous constellation of emotions and termed them "shame affects." He noted that the content of shame clusters around six themes: (i) I am weak; (ii) I am dirty and am looked at with disgust; (iii) I am defective; (iv) I lack control over my mind and body; (v) I am sexually excited by suffering and degradation, and (vi) I fear that showing myself will result in mockery and punishment. Shame affects can be overt or covert and can serve as screens against deeper anxieties (e.g., castration, separation). On the other hand, shame itself can be defended against by reactive grandiosity, induction of shame into others, depersonalization, and masochistic flaunting of degradation. Wurmser distinguished shame and guilt on two grounds: (i) shame is felt in a split form: about the *function* of self-exposure and about the *content* of what is exposed, but guilt has no such inner division; (ii) shame is deeper and more self-oriented while guilt is the experience of a more coherent ego and is fundamentally object-related. He stated that "Teleologically, shame may be important as the protector of primary process thought—the language of the self. Guilt may fulfil the same purpose for secondary process thought—the language of object relations" (p. 67).

Morrison (1989) also regarded shame as essentially related to the self-experience, hence inadequately conceptualized in the language of the tripartite structural model. He felt that a consideration of identity and the self was central to shame; indeed, "Shame is a crucial dysphoric affect in narcissistic phenomena" (p. 8). Morrison noted that:

> There is an ongoing, tension-generating dialectic between narcissistic grandiosity and desire for perfection, and the archaic sense of self as flawed, inadequate and inferior following the realization of separateness from, and dependence upon, objects. Similarly, a metaphorical dialectic exists between the wish for absolute autonomy and uniqueness and the wish for perfect merger and reunion with the projected fantasy of the ideal. Thus, shame and narcissism inform each other, as the self is experienced first, alone, separate, and small, and, again, grandiosely, striving to be perfect and re-united with its ideal. (p. 66)

Citing Kohut's (1971, 1977) later views on shame but differing from them, Morrison asserted that shame reflects primarily a selfobject failure to meet the age-appropriate needs of the self, especially those of the self striving to achieve vigor through attainment of its ideals.

Finally, in a series of papers, Lansky (1991, 1994, 1999, 2000, 2003a, 2003b, 2004, 2005, 2007) highlighted a number of issues pertaining to shame. These included (i) shame resulting from the individual's sense of being incapable of sustaining meaningful relationships; (ii) the relationship between shame, narcissistic rage, and suicide; (iii) the central relationship of shame to core self-experience, not just the self's actions; (iv) the causation of inner shame by the awareness of increased neediness for human contact; (v) the role of covert shame in struggles over forgiveness; (vi) shame-related conflicts as instigators of dreams, and (vii) the paradox that acknowledgement of shame arouses more shame and the role of this paradox in driving shame underground.

Synthesis

Pooling the foregoing observations and deleting their antiquated and incorrect parts (especially those pertaining to gender and sexuality), one can safely conclude that shame refers to a dysphoric affect with the following components: (i) collapse of self-esteem, (ii) feeling of humiliation, (iii) rupture of self-continuity, (iv) sense of isolation and disjunction from the surround, and (v) feeling of being watched by critical others, especially those from the peer group. Shame is similar to guilt insofar as both emotions cause distress and lower self-esteem. Both can act as guarantors of "appropriate" behaviors on the one hand, and both can drive one to self-laceration and suicide on the other. However, their differences are more marked than their similarities and include the following: (i) shame is visual, guilt auditory; (ii) shame is related to conflicts regarding exhibitionism, guilt to conflicts regarding transgression; (iii) shame is self-focused, guilt object-related; (iv) shame has physiological markers (e.g., blushing, palpitations), guilt does not; (v) shame results from failure to live up to a cherished self-image, guilt from disobeying actual or internalized authority; (vi) in structural terms, shame is a consequence of tension between ego and ego ideal while guilt is the result of tension between ego and superego; (vii) shame is developmentally earlier than guilt; (viii) shame pushes for hiding, guilt for confession, and (ix) defenses against shame include narcissistic self-inflation, social withdrawal, and shaming others; defenses against guilt include blaming others, fearing external punishment, and masochistic self-laceration. Having brought together the major psychoanalytic observations on shame in a harmonious gestalt, we are now prepared to address its absence.

Shamelessness

The dictionary definition of being "shameless" includes phrases like "having no shame" and "insensible to disgrace" (*Merriam-Webster's Collegiate Dictionary*, 1998, p. 1076). The first phrase is hardly informative. The second phrase tells us more. Implying that the individual who is shameless does not feel disgrace, it presents a portrait of social indifference. The shameless individual can express thoughts and opinions, use language, commit acts, and behave in ways that would send shivers of embarrassment over the spines of "civilized folk." He can belch, fart, and pick his nose with impunity. He can use foul language with a sailor's ease. He can ask favors upon favors without the slightest trepidation. He can give voice, with little hesitation, to his innermost fantasies including those of grandiosity and perverse sexuality. The shameless person seems to know no limits or, at least, not to care about any.

Drawn with such broad strokes, the nosological icon degrades into a caricature of ill-mannered psychopathy. In actuality, the phenomenon of shamelessness appears in myriad forms. These include, on the *normative pole* of the phenomenological spectrum: (i) development-based shamelessness, and (ii) dignity-based shamelessness, and on the *pathological pole*: (iii) defense-based shamelessness, (iv) discharge-based shamelessness, and (v) defect-based shamelessness. A brief comment on each form follows.

Development-based shamelessness

Although a modicum of "social referencing" (Emde, 1991) is evident in the infant from the earliest days, the experience of shame does not appear till the third year of life (Erikson, 1950). This is understandable in light of the foregoing consideration of shame which demonstrated that the capacity to experience shame is dependent upon a clear self-object discrimination and the "forward projection of narcissism" (Chasseguet-Smirgel, 1984, p. 28) resulting in the formation of the "ego ideal" (Freud, 1914c). In other words, for shame to be experienced, there ought to be a "shamed" and a "shamer" present *and* there should be some sense that one has fallen in the eyes of idealized others and below the ideal view of oneself. These capacities arise over childhood development and so does the capacity to experience shame. Parental upholding of the ideals that the child must aspire to and parental vulnerability to shame over this or that specific matter also contribute to the child's acquisition of the content-based sector of shame (i.e., *what* to be ashamed of).

Not surprisingly, Freud (1905d) attributed[2] the little child's polymorphous perverse sexuality to the fact that in him "mental dams against sexual excess—shame, disgust, and morality—have either not yet been constructed at all or are only in course of construction" (p. 191). However, even in the child, it is not an "either-or" issue; the capacity for shame can develop and yet certain areas might remain outside of its reign for quite some time.

Fart and awe

A fellow psychoanalyst, Patricia O'Neil (a pseudonym, of course) relayed the following incident to me. She was playing, on the floor, with her beloved grandson, Tommy. Getting up to go to the bathroom, she emitted a loud and prolonged fart. The three-year-old stopped his play, looked up at Patricia, and said with earnest glee, "That was great, Grammy! How did you do it?!" He felt no trepidation in commenting upon my colleague's admirable "skill."

Such absence of shame can be termed "development-based shamelessness." Or, following precedence evident in terms like "un-pleasure" (Freud, 1915e), and "un-fear" (Akhtar, 2012), it can be designated as "un-shame".[3]

Dignity-based shamelessness

It might, at first, seem preposterous to propose that shamelessness can occur in the setting of "dignity".[4] However, a contemplative pause might ease our way to seeing that this is not only possible but actually inevitable. Wurmser (1989) talked about "the 'shamelessness' of poets and scientists" (p. 52) and added that:

The less vulnerable one feels about ordinarily threatened parts of the self, or in more technical terms, the more solid and conflict-free the narcissistic investment, the self-valuation, becomes the less one will fear exposure, and hence shame. If we are confident of the value of our life as a whole, of its integrity and true wholeness, as we can assume Einstein and Freud were, we have less need to shield it against self-exposure. (p. 52)

The following incident, involving Gandhi, reported by Lapierre and Collins (1975) in their book on India's independence struggle, *Freedom at Midnight*, testifies to this type of healthy and glowing shamelessness.

The yogurt of reciprocity

While visiting Lord Mountbatten (then the Governor General of India) upon his invitation to discuss some political matters, Gandhi was offered a cup of tea and some biscuits by the towering British figure. Gandhi accepted the offer and then produced a small container of yogurt that had been wrapped in his loin-cloth and forwarded it to Mountbatten, saying that the exchange of delicacies must be reciprocal.

Such proud and courageous forthrightness carries along with itself a certain sense of freedom from shame. Curiously, while the scientist and the leader feel *no need* to hide their conviction and hence are shameless, the writer and poet *render* the deeply private and conflicted into dignified forms and thus make the inner goings-on shameless. Nietzsche (1886) said it most clearly: "The poets are shameless about their experiences; they exploit them" (p. 161). A more recent exposition of the same thought comes from Allen Wheelis (1975) that has the creative writer tell us the following:

My uniqueness must slip effortlessly into others' minds and there clone itself, my singularity then appear in the experience of everyone, spring up everywhere, like April flowers. What I lived alone in hideous idiosyncracy and pain will now be lived by all in acceptance and mutuality. I will have fathered the world; like God, will have created it in my own image. I create self, defiantly from the winds of contingency, then claim universality by extending that contingency to the furthermost limits of the known world. (pp. 82–83)

Thus the transformation of potentially shame-laden mental contents into a literary product yields aesthetic pleasure for all and confers dignity upon the creative writer (Freud, 1908b). He has nothing to hide anymore and through a circuitous route, joins the fraternity of healthy shamelessness of which the bold politician is already a proud member.

Defense-based shamelessness

Vulnerability to shame can, at times, be handled by counterphobic mechanisms. Fenichel (1945) mentioned a case where the attitude of shamelessness was a reaction to a preceding period strongly laden with shame. Wurmser (1981) also talked of the apparent shamelessness of sexual exhibitionists being a counterphobic operation against shame. He added that social exhibitionists and professional actors might utilize the same defense. Instead of being a regression to a psychic state before the establishment of the shame barrier, shamelessness, according to Wurmser, is the outcome of a complex layer of defenses.

> The shameless person is a variant of the "criminal from a sense of guilt" who commits a crime so he can feel guilty for and expiate some known and clearly defined misdeed rather than remaining saddled with a vague, shapeless inner guilt about unconscious wishes. It could be viewed as a "reaction formation against reaction formation"—a brazen violation of a taboo to defend against guilt, which in turn has been set upon a defense against the violation of a much deeper taboo. Similarly shamelessness is a reaction formation against shame, which in turn is a reaction formation against delophilic and theatophilic[5] wishes. Superficially, it simply appears as shame displaced. (p. 261)

Such shamelessness comes to serve as a transparent fig leaf against the dreaded experience of genuine shame. Individuals with the syndrome of "malignant narcissism" (Kernberg, 1984) display such defensive shamelessness. They seek to destroy whatever love is offered to them and declare that they are above the need for attachment and affection. Lurking underneath this cold superiority is "the shame of not having been loved" (Kjellqvist, 1993, p. 11) during childhood.[6]

Discharge-based shamelessness

Shamelessness can also serve the purpose of instinctual discharge. If a particular partial instinct (e.g., exhibitionism, sadism, masochism) is too strong, then it can override the customary barrier of shame; being shameless then facilitates the expression of the drive.[7] While this relationship was first noted by Freud (1905d) in the context of sexual perversion, it is also evident in the course of a "healthy" erotic encounter. Shedding one's shame over nakedness and gently overcoming the partner's shame are important constituents during foreplay (Kernberg, 1991a). Anxieties regarding real and imaginary blemishes of one's body have to be put aside and this, in turn, requires genuine self-regard and trust in the partner's goodness. Another important aspect of foreplay is the emergence into consciousness of pregenital drive directives (e.g., sucking, licking, biting, looking, showing, smelling) and their spontaneous expression needs to be shame-free in order to be pleasurable. Sexual intercourse too involves postures, acts, demands, and verbalizations that, outside of such context, could be regarded as shameful. In the context of erotic union, however, they are not; a robust and playful shamelessness prevails.

Discharge-based shamelessness can be witnessed in other realms as well. The drive to perform well (and therefore, win the love of real or imaginary others) in certain professions (e.g., striptease dancing, acting, salesmanship) can tip the balance of drive-defense in favour of the former and make shamelessness a psychic "wingman" of desire. At times, the environment can stir up longings that become too irresistible and lead to their shameless expression.

The director's plea

During my college days, I used to act on stage. Once, as the play ended, one of my fellow actors walked out on the stage and announced that all the credit should go to the play's director, Mr Mehra. Then, in the characteristically Anglicized manner of those days, he boomed, "Three cheers for Mr Mehra! Hip hip hooray, hip hip hooray, hip hip hooray!" A year later, I was again in the college play but this time with a new director, Mr Gupta, at the helm. Just as the play was ending and actors were lining up to walk on the stage for a curtain call, I felt someone tap on my shoulder. It was Mr Gupta, who whispered to me, "Like last year's cheers for Mr Mehra, can you say the same words for me today?" Drenched in the sweat of embarrassment at the old man's desperate hunger to be admired (and, his naked competitiveness), I was dumbfounded and could not utter those words once I was on the stage. He never forgave me for that!

Defect-based shamelessness

This type of shamelessness is found in the setting of severely narcissistic and antisocial personality organizations. According to Wurmser (1981), "Certain aspects of their self have become so dissociated and unimportant that they can be exposed without narcissistic pain" (p. 138).[8] Freud's (1914c) evocation of a truly hardened criminal for illustrating the smugness of primary narcissism is also a case in point here. And, it is true that the narcissistic person, especially the one with antisocial tendencies, can "shamelessly" make demands upon others' love, time, and material resources. The unconscious envy and hostility towards the benefactor is often striking under such circumstances.

The curious fate of a compliment

> Catherine McCarthy, a thirty-seven-year-old attorney with a pronounced tendency to be flirtatious that arose from a powerful oedipal fixation, narrated the following incident during one of her analytic sessions with me. She said that the previous evening, she had given a compliment to her highly successful and narcissistic husband regarding his handling of the family dog. "You are far better with Jake [the dog] than I am," she had said. With disbelief and pain in her voice, she then told that he responded to her admiring comment by saying, "Darling, I am better than you in most things."

Whether one chooses to say anything about this remark or not, it seems clear that my patient's husband had difficulty accepting and enjoying his wife's "goodness" towards him. Her comment stirred up greed instead of gratitude in him; envy of her capacity for kindness perhaps also played a role in his devaluing remark. In addition to all this, there was a quality of shamelessness to her husband's self-centered boasting.

Sociocultural dimension

Since shame and shamelessness are essentially relational phenomena that arise from the era of early childhood, they inevitably become culture-bound in their prevalence, intensity, and the affected sectors of fantasy and behavior. Indeed, the phrase "cultures of shame" has been around for quite some time and is intended to categorize some societies from others that are viewed as "cultures of guilt." Kitayama (2007) employs the term "shame culture," for instance, to designate the Japanese society which regards "life as a drama in which actors wear fragile masks" (p. 93). He goes on to state that:

> Anxieties about shame become stronger when their masks are stripped away and their real faces are exposed .... In the psychology of the awareness of shame, as Kenichero Okano (1998) states, it is easy to understand if we regard the self as carrying the duality of an "ideal self" and a "shameful self." It may be correct to differentiate the two by calling the former the adaptive self or the public self, and the latter the true self or the private self (Kitayama, 2004). This duality is repeatedly described in ordinary Japanese language, such as *omoto* to *ura* (front and back), *homae* to *tatemae* (what one says and what one means), and *giani* to *ninjo* (duty and sentiment). (p. 93, italics in the original)

With variations in nuance and focus, similar proclivity of preserving one's public appearance at all costs prevails in many other cultures in Asia, especially, perhaps, the Islamic nations. Shame—or its dreaded anticipation—underlies "honor killings" prevalent in the less literate sections of these societies; the exposure of a transgression (especially by a female member of the family) is deemed worse than the transgression itself, and is to be strenuously avoided. Shamelessness in such settings can be fatal.

It is conventional to contrast such "cultures of shame" with the "cultures of guilt" which presumably inculcate greater respect for rules and give lesser weight to the fear of public exposure in the course of moral development. To be sure, such juxtaposition can have some heuristic yield but it carries the stale odor of Western colonialization which views its foundational structures to be superior. A more stark contrast might actually be between "cultures of shame" and "cultures of shamelessness." Talking specifically of the United States, Hoffer (1974) declared that "We have become a shameless society ... the loss of shame threatens our survival as a civilized society" (p. D-4). Christopher Lasch (1971) bemoaned such a "culture of narcissism" and Lowenfeld (1976) observed:

> Nowadays, even the bikini is often replaced by a thin string. Where formerly patients, even in analytic treatment, had severe inhibitions

about speaking of their masturbatory practices and overcame their shame only against strong resistance, now lovers chat with each other about their masturbatory practices. Specially manufactured vibrators are displayed in the windows of reputable drug-stores. "Porno" literature and movies of polymorphous-perverse practices, once checked by shame, are now devoured by civilized people. The use of obscene language, mocking old fashioned feelings, has become quite general. (p. 67)

Shamelessness—whether era-bound or geographically located—can indeed raise a cross-cultural "confusion of tongues" (Ferenczi, 1933), so to speak.[9] What might appear normal and acceptable behavior in one culture can seem quite shameless to an observer who hails from a different culture. Look at the following examples.

A tourist woman from Saudi Arabia (accompanied, of course, by her husband and/or other family members) happens to see a young American girl wearing a bikini on a beach and instinctively regards the latter as shameless. But is the American girl really shameless?

A British couple invites a Pakistani friend to dinner. The latter asks if he can bring along his elderly father, who's visiting from their ancestral village. The hosts extend their hospitality to the older man who emits a loud and extended belch after the dinner. He regards that belch as an expression of his gustatory gratitude while the British couple blushes with shame on his behalf!

An Iranian physician who is residing and practicing in New York returns to Shiraz for a visit. During one festive dinner, his deceased father's friend asks him—in sight and hearing of all present—how much money he makes every month. The Iranian doctor, who has become quite Westernized by now, finds the old man's inquiry to be intrusive but out of respect, decides to answer anyway. Upon receiving this answer, the old man turns and loudly announces the figure to all present. This the young Iranian physician finds to be a shameless act.

A female physician from the repressive and "proper" Tamil Brahmin community in Chennai feels horrified when, on her first day of internship in

Chicago, she hears an American medical student say that he has done a "very good" write-up on his patient. She cannot fathom how one can praise oneself openly and finds the student to be utterly shameless.

These vignettes reveal that a considerable portion of the shame affect is context-bound, needs a shamed-shamer dyad, and is open to influence by the ethos of the two parties. All this, of course, has relevance to the conduct of psychotherapy and psychoanalysis.

Technical implications

By its nature, psychoanalytic treatment involves uncovering the prohibited, the transgressive, the infantile, and the profane, hidden in unlit corners of the mind. Patients might seek help for rational concerns (e.g., work-inhibition, sexual problems) and begin treatment with thorough elaborations of their complaints and by expressing sincere hopes for getting over them. Sooner or later, however, the cognitive sieve of free association permits the leakage of the seemingly irrational and the hitherto unknown material into the discourse. Secrets, long held deliberately, and fantasies that were repressed and "forgotten" now begin to surface. Shame enters the clinical chamber and self-revelation falters.

Clinical vignette: 1

Jules Levin, a fledgling businessman in his late forties, had a painful childhood. Born with a visible deformity of his face, he was also short of stature. Throughout his childhood, he was mocked by his father and, over time, became acutely vulnerable to shame. He started keeping his thoughts and actions secret. One secret that came out early in his treatment was his sexually touching his younger sister while she was fast asleep; this began when Jules was eleven years old and lasted for a few months. In reporting his late night excursions to me, Jules felt shame but was unable to recall (or speculate about) his fantasies and expectations in doing this. He simply felt he had to do something odd, something bizarre, to have an alive psychic self since his normal self had been decimated by his cruel father (and ignored by his mother).

During one session, while talking freely about how he sought vitality in lieu of his depressive existence, he suddenly stopped. Something had clearly come to his mind that was difficult to talk about. With gentle interpretation of his fears of my reaction, Jules became able to talk again. He revealed that he has the shameful habit of picking his nose and then eating his snot. I could sense a profound sense of sadness and solitude connected to Jules's behavior. I responded by saying that there seemed to be some connection between his touching his sister's genitals and his eating his snot; a certain audacity characterized both these behaviors. My voice was peaceful and conveyed my deep interest in his emotional life. Jules relaxed and began talking more fluently.

Since shame is invariably diminished by calm acceptance by the onlooker (or, the "on-listener"), the therapist's nonjudgmental "holding" (Winnicott, 1960a, 1960b) goes a long way in strengthening the therapeutic alliance. This is true in instances where the patient is consciously experiencing the dread of being shamed but also applies to situations where he or she is not even cognizant that a particular behavior has the potential of becoming shameful.

Clinical vignette: 2

At the end of a session in the second month of her analysis, Melanie Wright, an otherwise psychologically minded young woman, offered me a bag full of apples. She said that she had gone apple-picking over the weekend and wanted me to have some. I was taken aback. Neither her characteristic way of being nor the material in the session had prepared me for this. I responded, "I appreciate your bringing me this gift but I cannot accept it. See, our task here is to understand, enlighten ourselves to your mental functioning and, thus, come to grips with your difficulties. We cannot, therefore, move into actions, especially ones whose meanings are unknown to us. Now, I regret if my stance hurts your feelings, but I do not apologise because my intent is not to hurt you." She listened carefully and nodded in agreement. I then spontaneously added, "For instance, apples. What comes to mind about apples?" She answered, "Adam's apple! … Adam and Eve … forbidden fruit." She smiled, blushed, and left shaking her head, saying, "I understand, I understand."

This vignette shows how the steadfast maintenance of a therapeutic frame and "invitation" for the patient to become more curious lays down the foundations of a good alliance. It also demonstrates that a sustained analytic attitude itself acts as a rescuer of the patient from the brink of shame.

This is not to say that the analyst himself is not vulnerable to shame. To be sure, healthy self-esteem, reasonably well-analysed personal conflicts, renunciation of omnipotent expectations from oneself, and availability of libidinal supplies protect the analyst from feeling shame in the course of his work. However, a patient in the throes of negative transference can readily demolish such resolve on the analyst's part, especially by attacking the latter's ethnicity, race, physical attributes, language proficiency, and technique. Feeling ashamed in response, the analyst can become defensive and, worse, retaliatory.

Besides such obvious triggers, analyst's shame can arise from associative recall of shameful experiences (old and new) outside his clinical life. And, at times, an inquiry from the patient that is in fact reflective of psychic growth can unexpectedly lead the analyst to encounter inner shame.

Clinical vignette: 3

A fifty-year-old Hindu Indian woman, Sunita Jha, had been raised by an instinctually repressed (and repressive) family in South Africa, and spoke mainly in English during her analysis. As early fears of criticism and rejection were interpretively softened, a devalued self-image emerged. While childhood experiences of prejudice due to skin color were emphasized at first, analysis gradually revealed profound rejection by her mother, a rejection centering upon her being female. Work along these lines relaxed her further and occasionally she began to speak in Hindi, her mother tongue. During one such session, Sunita very hesitantly revealed that she did not know the word for the female genital in Hindi and felt that it would help her to acquire this knowledge. Issues of maternal transference (i.e., can I label her body parts for her?; do I know and accept that she has female genitalia?; do I accept "my" female genitalia?, etc.) were clearly evident and I handled them in the customary analytic fashion.

However, in a later session, she quite earnestly asked me to tell her the word. Suddenly I found myself experiencing a dual dilemma. One was a purely technical dilemma in the sense of what would be the process-related pros and cons of telling her the word as against inquiring as to why she wanted to know it from me, and so on. The other dilemma which caught me by surprise involved my overall etiquette of life, as it were. Can I even utter the word in my mother tongue (spoken Hindi and Urdu have the same word for the female genital) in the presence of a woman? Or, would I feel ashamed while doing so? Experiencing the inhibition outlined nearly a century ago by Ferenczi (1911), for a moment, I became tongue-tied.[10] Then working through the inner block and in the spirit of "developmental work" (Pine, 1997) that includes occasionally providing patients with words for what is hard for them to express, I decided to tell her that it was called *choot*.

While this was a homoethnic clinical dyad, problems of the sort highlighted by it tend to occur with greater frequency in cross-cultural analyses (Platt, 2015). A culturally different patient's pointing out that the analyst has been mispronouncing his name, or the name of the city he came from, can cause embarrassment to the analyst. And then there are narcissistic patients who are extremely prone to feeling ashamed and hardly need cultural pressure points to deposit their shame-laden self-representations (by projective identification) into the analyst. The latter's characterological resistance to shame, his capacity to contain such projections, and his ability to feel (and yet keep in abeyance) his sadistic desires to shame such patients, constitute important therapeutic tools in clinical work of this stripe.

Conclusion

In this contribution, I have provided a brief survey of the psychoanalytic literature on shame and, based upon that, delineated the affective and cognitive characteristics of this experience. I have, however, devoted greater attention to the absence (actual or seeming) of shame and have categorized such shamelessness into five types: (i) development-based, (ii) defense-based, (iii) discharge-based, (iv) defect-based, and (v) dignity-based. By carving out the first and last categories, I have rescued shamelessness from being regarded as necessarily pathological. Moving on, I have discussed the sociocultural dimensions of shamelessness and also addressed issues pertaining to it in the clinical situation. This has been a tedious but rewarding sojourn and has imparted an important lesson, namely that while Euripides (circa 413 BC) called shamelessness "the worst of human diseases" (p. 37), it can also exist in the setting of a child's innocence and a great man's self-assurance. Thus not only shame but shamelessness, too, turns out to be a multi-determined, context-based, and complex phenomenon. In acknowledging that matters in this realm are not straightforward, one need feel no shame at all.

CHAPTER FIVE

Regret

C ertain affects have the peculiar quality of linking the temporal characteristics of the system *Cs* and the system *Ucs* (Freud, 1915e). They pointedly exist in the present but are content-wise totally involved with the past. Remorse is one such emotion and regret the other. The former, though often conflated with guilt (Klein, 1935, 1940), has received considerable attention from psychoanalysts. The latter has not. The index to the Standard Edition of Freud's complete works contains no entry on "regret." The five major dictionaries of psychoanalysis (Eidelberg, 1968; Laplanche & Pontalis, 1973; Moore & Fine, 1968, 1990; Rycroft, 1968) also do not mention "regret". The PEP Web, the electronic compendium of psychoanalytic literature spanning 116 years and containing nearly 90,000 entries, lists one single paper (Kavaler-Adler, 2004) with the word "regret" in its title. It is therefore clear that despite its being ubiquitous and troubling, regret as an emotion has received almost no attention within our literature.

My contribution here is aimed to fill this gap. I will begin my consideration of "regret" with delineating its phenomenological characteristics and differentiating it from the related affect of remorse. I will then trace the origins of regret and attempt to demonstrate the intricate scenarios of ontogenesis and "actual" missteps of adult life that undergird it.

Following this, I will make a brief sociocultural foray and then address the clinical implications of the proposals made so far. I will conclude by summarizing and synthesizing the diverse material in this contribution and by noting areas that merit further investigation.

Etymology, definition, and phenomenology

The current English word "regret" is derived from the addition of prefix "re" to the Old German or Old Norse word *greter*, which meant "to weep." Regret thus originally meant "to weep again." This etymological nuance is, however, restricted to the hyphenated form (i.e., "re-gret") of the word which has largely become extinct in contemporary English though still mentioned in certain dictionaries. There the definitions of "re-gret" and "regret" appear different. "Re-gret" is defined as "(i) a: to mourn the loss or death of, b: to miss very much; (ii) to be very sorry for," and "regret" as "(i) sorrow aroused by circumstances beyond one's control or power to repair, (ii) a: an expression of distressing emotions (as sorrow or disappointment); b: a note politely declining an invitation" (*Merriam-Webster Collegiate Dictionary*, 1993, p. 985). Of note here is that the temporal implication of the old "re-gret" is obfuscated, if not entirely lost, by "regret" which entered the English language in the late sixteenth century. Compare this to the stunning poem "Regret" by Charlotte Brontë (1816–1855) and the moorings of the emotions in events past shall become unmistakably evident. I will cite the entire poem later in this essay and restrict myself here to declaring that this poem is a treasure trove of insights about the emotion of regret. It subsumes the role of intentionality and agency, loss, wistfulness, nostalgia, and desperate wish to undo what one has done—all under the throbbing rubric of regret.

This leads me to the psychoanalytic perspective on regret. Kavaler-Adler (2004), the only author to have written a psychoanalytic paper on regret, states that "[R]emorse and regret interweave intra-psychically" (p. 40). In my *Comprehensive Dictionary of Psychoanalysis* (Akhtar, 2009), I elucidated the overlaps and distinctions between the two emotions in the following manner.

> "Regret" shares many features with its twin sister, "remorse" (see separate entry). Both are about the past. Both are about one's own actions. Both can involve acts of commission or omission. Both lead

to a wistful rumination to somehow erase or undo the events of the past. Both can, therefore, underlie the "if only" fantasies. This fantasy assumes that, in the absence of this or that "calamity," everything would have turned out alright. Both "regret" and "remorse" can impoverish the ego and contribute to anhedonia, depression, and suicidal tendencies. Finally, both "regret" and "remorse" can serve screen functions and both can be put to secondary (e.g., sadomasochistic) uses. However, there is one very important difference between the two emotions: "remorse" involves feelings about how one's actions have affected others, while "regret" involves feelings about how one's actions affected oneself. In other words, "remorse" is more object related, "regret" more narcissistic. (2009, p. 244)

Elaborating on these concise remarks, I now suggest that regret is a complex, dysphoric state that can be situation-based and fleeting or characterologically anchored and sustained. It can be about actions that had an unfortunate outcome or it can be about acts not undertaken and opportunities missed. Here, I disagree with the philosopher, Irving Thalberg (1963), who suggests that personal responsibility is a defining feature of remorse while only a characteristic feature of regret. In his view, regret can arise about events that one had little control over (e.g., the passing of summer). My counterpoint is that even such events are "personalized" in the unconscious of the regretful individual; he might think: "A! The summer passed and I did nothing to enjoy it." This causes him distress. In fact, there is some evidence that the distress arising from acts of omission is often greater than that from acts of commission (Kahneman & Tversky, 1982).

Chronic regret also includes intricate disturbances of ego and superego functioning. The impaired ego functions are evident via loss of flexibility in considering matters of the inner world and external reality and disturbances in the subjective experience of time which seems to have stopped, and masochistic submission to a life in bondage. Cognition is flooded with "contrafactual thought, or imagining states contrary to the fact: especially what might have been" (Landman, 1993, p. 37). The superego disturbances include hyper-criticism of past actions (or inactions) and their (real or imaginary) consequences and lack of self-forgiveness, a mockingly triumphant attitude towards the hapless sectors of the ego, and a clever jettisoning of current pleasures at the altar of ever-unachievable peace in life at present. Linking the ego and superego reactions is the wish to undo the past decisions that have turned out to be self-damaging. Lady Macbeth's handwashing is a well-known example of an act intended to magically expunge something that was done in the past.

At times, a well systematized "if only ..." fantasy comes to dominate the mind. Elsewhere, I have elaborated upon the psychic constellation of this fantasy in the following words:

> Individuals with the "if only ..." fantasy lack interest in the future and constantly wring their hands over something that happened in the past. They insist that if only it had not taken place, everything would have turned out (or would have been) all right. Life before that event is glossed over or retrospectively idealized. When a child-hood event, for example, parental divorce, gets involved in the "if only ..." fantasy, an elaborate "personal myth" (Kris, 1956) tends to develop that, with its seductive logic, might even go unquestioned during analytic treatment (e.g., my case of Mr. A. in Kramer & Akhtar, 1988). The "screen" nature of such "if only ..." formula-tions, however, is clearer when the trauma, relentlessly harped on, is from the recent past. Individuals who remain tormented year after year by the memories of a failed romance from college days, a psychotherapist who moved out of town, or an extramarital lover who withdrew his or her affection often give histories of having been painfully "dropped" from maternal attention during early childhood. (Akhtar, 1999b, p. 222).

Those afflicted with chronic regret claim to be suffering from the narcissistic depletion consequent upon "bad" decisions of their past. An impulsive marriage, a reckless resignation from a job, an abrupt emigration, a hasty purchase of a house, and a thoughtless abortion are the sort of themes that preoccupy them. To be sure, any and all such events can lead to adverse consequences and to a retrospective wish to undo the decision, which is a central feature of regret. However, matters are not as simple as they appear. Careful scrutiny invariably reveals that not all their current suffering is due to the alleged "wrong turn" taken years ago. Even more important, the regretful individual remains focused upon the consequences of his earlier decisions and shows little curiosity about the potential origins of that decision. In other words, the fact that something already problematic in his psyche might have propelled that "bad" decision is completely ignored.

Developmental origins and later elaborations

Exploration of the development background of such individuals often reveals earlier wounds that have resulted in a generalized or focal self-care deficiency and/or to unconscious masochism. Their inability to be vigilant and self-protective while making important decisions had arisen from early maternal neglect; they simply do not feel valuable and worthy of loving care, even by themselves. Their masochistic surrender to a rejecting mother (and perhaps also a similar father) had led to an inner imperative to dissipate themselves and act in irresponsible ways.

A concomitant to the resulting regret is inactivity and chronic waiting to be put together right all over again. Abraham (1924a) made the following astute comment pertaining to such dynamics:

> Some people are dominated by the belief that there will always be some kind person—a representative of the mother of course—to care for them and to give them everything they need. This optimistic belief condemns them to inactivity. (p. 399)

The optimism that Abraham refers to exists on a covert basis in the regretful person. In a disguised and chronologically inverted manner, such hopefulness pops up in the form of nostalgia. The wish to capture an idealized past and an admixture of pain and joy characterizes this emotional state. Pain is evoked by awareness of separation from the now idealized object and joy by a fantasied reunion with it through reminiscences. "It is the subtlety, iridescence, and ambivalence of these feelings that gives nostalgia its inimitable coloration" (Werman, 1977, p. 393). While often attributed to a loss during adult life, this characteristically "bitter-sweet pleasure" (Kleiner, 1970, p. 11) has its origin in the incomplete mourning of a traumatic disruption of the early mother–child relationship. Sterba (1940) was the first to correlate homesickness with a longing for the maternal breast. Fenichel (1945) also explained nostalgia as a wish to return to the preoedipal mother. Fodor (1950) went so far as to correlate nostalgic yearning with a deep-seated longing for the undisturbed prenatal state. However, these references to prenatal bliss, maternal breast, and preoedipal mother are better regarded as largely metaphorical. Much takes place between a premature traumatic rupture of the infantile bliss and its alleged counterpart in adulthood. Hartmann's (1955) warning regarding the "genetic fallacy" must be heeded here. Recall of such early events is questionable, fantasies involving them are retrospective creations, and the idealization is intended to keep aggressively tinged self- and object representations in abeyance. It is, however, unmistakable that the nostalgic individual is looking for a completely untroubled state. Such a person is looking not only for the lost object but for an idealized object and, even more important, for the time before the object was lost.

The accompanying "if only ..." fantasy is a product of incomplete mourning over the loss of the all-good mother of symbiosis. It expresses a position whereby the idealized primary object is neither given up through the work of grieving nor assimilated into the ego through identification. Instead, the object is retained in psychic limbo by a stubborn nostalgic relationship which is:

> ... characteristically indeterminate in its representations, and by its imaginary nature the subject is able to maintain separateness from the object. This leads to an indefinite and indefinable quest—and if an object should appear that seems to correspond to the nostalgic desire, it is promptly rejected, it becomes demythologized; it is not what it promised to be: the subject's projection of what it should be. The subject can thus only enjoy the search and never the possession. (Werman, 1977, p. 391)

At the same time, the displaced derivatives of this "loss" are harped on ad infinitum. Splitting mechanisms also play a significant role here since the aggressively tinged representations of the lost object are totally repudiated and/or displaced onto other objects.

The nostalgic yearning for the past often coexists with the "someday ..." fantasy which propels excessive hope on an overt basis, and a relentless search for ideal conditions. Individuals with the "if only ... fantasy live in the past and those with the "someday ..." fantasy live in the future; both are alienated from the present. A temporal fracture of this kind is central to the experience of regret. Even the regret of the elderly that they did not devote enough time to their families when their children were young is often a shield against the horror of realizing that they ended up becoming like their own busy and neglectful parents. The "old" past gets buried in the poisoned garden of the "new" past and the self is cleaved in time.[1]

Sociocultural vicissitudes

The emotion of regret with its characteristics of hand-wringing and masochistic self-laceration is a captivating theme for fiction and poetry. Proust's (1871–1922) *Remembrance of Things Past,* written between 1912 and 1921, might have a greater dose of mourning and nostalgia but does contain a dollop of regret as well. Four prominent illustrations of regret in modern fiction are the following:

> Ernest Hemingway's short story, *The Snows of Kilimanjaro* (1936), which has a protagonist who has lived a life of sloth and procrastination whose full-of-promise past has ended up in a harrowing present of despair. Erosion of values pervades the tale: loose sex, lost love, revenge, war, and heavy drinking.

> Joseph Heller's (1966) novel, *Something Happened,* which is a meandering saga of a middle-aged mid-level executive who feels directionless, bored, and morose, but inwardly clings to the "hope" represented by the innocent and unconsummated passion he felt for a girl when he was a teenager, a girl who committed suicide long ago.

> Louis Begley's (1993) novel, *The Man Who Was Late,* which describes the life of a middle-aged investment banker who masks his existential angst by an opulent lifestyle but lets his undue vigilance and lack of faith in human bonds torpedo his last chance for fulfilling love. His preexisting sense of isolation is compounded by the ensuing regret and leads to his suicide.

> Julian Barnes's (2013) novella, *The Sense of an Ending,* which is a meditation on memory, aging, and how perverse permutations of human choices can cause enormous damage and inconsolable remorse and regret.

To be sure, more examples can be given from the world of fiction.[2] A far greater impression, however, is made by the poetry pertaining to the emotion of regret. I have earlier in this discussion referred to Charlotte Brontë's (1846) poem, "Regret." Here I quote it in its entirety.

Long ago I wished to leave
"The house where I was born;"
Long ago I used to grieve,
My home seemed so forlorn.
In other years, its silent rooms
Were filled with haunting fears;
Now, their very memory comes
O'er charged with tender tears.
Life and marriage I have known,
Things once deemed so bright;
Now, how utterly is flown
Every ray of light!
Mid the unknown sea of life
I no blest isle have found;
At last, through all its wild wave's strife,
My bark is homeward bound.
Farewell, dark and rolling deep!
Farewell, foreign shore!
Open, in unclouded sweep,
Thou glorious realm before!
Yet, though I had safely pass'd
That weary, vexed main,
One loved voice, through surge and blast,
Could call me back again
Though the soul's bright morning rose
O'er Paradise for me,
William! even from Heaven's repose
I'd turn, invoked by thee!
Storm nor surge should e'er arrest
My soul, exulting then:
All my heaven was once thy breast,
Would it were mine again!

The opening two lines of the poem tell it all. The first line, "Long ago I wished to leave," lays down the anachronistic foundation of things to come; it all began elsewhere, in some other time, the poet declares. The second line, "The house where I was born," is rendered within double quotation marks as if to remind the reader that he may or may not have been born in that particular house or to nudge the poet into an imp-ish complicity with a "personal myth" (Kris, 1956). Starting from these lines, the poem goes on to idealization, search, failure to find a haven, and ultimately a "psychic retreat" (Steiner, 1993) of confession and nostalgia: "All my heaven was once thy breast, would it were mine again." That Brontë titled a poem of futile choices, loss, wistful longing, and retrospective idealization "Regret" (without ever using the word itself in the body of the poem) testifies not only to her artistic savvy but to her deep psychological grasp of the experience of regret. While this poem is exemplary, good poems on regret must exist in other languages. I, for one, am aware of the striking poem, *Humesha der kar deta hoon maiN*, by Munir Niazi (1986) in Urdu, which bemoans the author's tendency to be late for all important occasions and how this causes him great pain.

An interesting point to note about the poems by Brontë and Niazi is that the affect of regret is intermingled with a bit of remorse in them. This is because both poets take their own self as an object and thus can "empathize" with its distress. The ensuing regret thus gets imbued with tenderness. This is what I call "warm regret".[3] In contrast to this is the "cold regret" where the self is not taken as an object and the concern remains purely narcissistic. The poem, "The Miser," by the Nobel Prize winning Indian poet, Rabindranath Tagore (1861–1941), is a depiction of the latter variety of regret.

> I had gone a begging from door to door in the village path,
> When thy golden chariot appeared in the distance
> Like a gorgeous dream and I wonder
> Who was the king of all kings!
>
> My hopes rose high and me thought
> My evil days were at an end,
> And I stood waiting for alms to be given unasked
> And for wealth scattered on all sides in the dust.
>
> The chariot stopped where I stood.
> Thy glance fell on me and thou camest down with a smile.
> I felt that the luck of my life had come at last.
> Then of a sudden thou didst hold thy right hand
> And say "What hast thou to give me?"
>
> Ah, what a kingly jest was it
> To open thy palm to a beggar to beg!
> I was confused and stood undecided,

And then from my wallet I slowly took out the least
Little grain of corn and gave it to thee.

But how great my surprise when at the day's end
I emptied my bag on the floor
To find a least little gram of gold among the poor heap.
I bitterly wept and wished that
I HAVE THE HEART TO GIVE THEE MY ALL. (1910, p. 58,
upper case used in the original)

Literature is not the only cultural vehicle for the expression of regret, however. Politics and social etiquette are other realms which involve both expression and denials of regret. In the political arena, remorse and regret often underlie strategic decisions and shifts in governmental policies. Responding to remorse, a nation can acknowledge its misdeeds and attempt to offer reparations; the affirmative action policies in the United States towards its racial minorities, the German reparations to Holocaust survivors, and the work of Bishop Desmond Tutu's Truth and Reconciliation Commission in South Africa are some illustrations of the beneficial political praxis catalysed by national remorse. Concern for the injustice done to others undergirds such operations. Regret is, however, a different thing altogether. Here a nation or a community feels that it has missed out on the opportunity to be supremely powerful, even omnipotent, and thus resorts to large-group nostalgia and fundamentalist attempts to revivify the preexisting (real or imagined) grandeur. Ex-Nazis reincarnating as the German skinheads, white supremacists in United States, Serbian nationalists of the 1990s, and the current radical Muslims (especially of the ISIS stripe) represent the political praxis of regret. Remorse seeks to repair a damaged object while regret attempts to restore narcissistic integrity.

A less virulent entry of regret into political arena is evident in its replacing the offer of apology. Politician after politician expresses "regret" at their misdeeds instead of apologizing. President Ronald Reagan stated the following as an "apology" for his selling arms to kidnappers linked to Iran who would release US hostages in return and would divert some funds to right-wing groups in Nicaragua the Reagan administration backed: "A few months ago, I told the American people I did not trade arms for hostages. My heart and my best intentions still tell me that's true, but the facts and the evidence tell me it's not .... It was a mistake" (cited in Battistella, 2014, p. 107). And, President Bill Clinton deftly transformed remorse into regret in the acknowledgement of his sexual liaison with the then nineteen-year-old Monica Lewinsky. He said "I know that my public comments and my silence about this matter gave a false impression. I misled people, including even my wife. I deeply regret that" (cited in James, 2013). The use of the word "regret" in the post-Donald Trump denunciation comment by US Supreme Court Justice Ruth Bader Ginsburg seems, on the other hand, well chosen and correct. She said, "On reflection, my recent remarks, i.e., response to press inquiries were ill-advised and I regret making them" (cited in Alvarez, 2016, p. 14). She was regretful but decidedly unapologetic.

The reluctance of political leaders to apologize is based upon both idealism and expedience. A leader is not supposed to be weak, after all; he must not admit to doing something hurtful to others though he might acknowledge having made a "mistake." Moreover, apologizing opens up the risk of the victim asking for reparations. Replacing apology by regret bypasses such "inconvenience." The ex-governor of Virginia, therefore, was willing to say that he "deeply regret(s) accepting illegal gifts and loans" (cited in Dockterman, 2014, p. 16) rather than that he was apologetic to his constituents. Similarly the wealthy investment banker, Tom Perkins said, "I regret the use of that word" when he retracted his comparison of popular attack on the richest one percent of Americans to being put in a "concentration camp" (cited in Takahashi, 2014). Statements of such sort are intended to wipe out a self-blemish; they do not reflect any concern for others.

Further dilution of "regret" is found in social discourse where one is almost relieved to "regret" not attending a cousin's brother-in-law's daughter's engagement party or an out-of-town ninetieth birthday of an ex-boss that would warrant considerable expenditure and would most likely be a dreadfully dull event. "Regret" under such circumstances is welcomed by the one expressing it. Conversely, the real estate colloquialism "buyer's remorse" should actually be "buyer's regret" since it has little to do with hurting the seller or the agent. All in all, in the chamber of language, regret, remorse, guilt, shame, counter-phobic confession, and expedient mendacity frequently masquerade each other. Such "sliding of meanings" (Horowitz, 1975) is also witnessed in clinical work with narcissistic individuals.

Technical implications

The treatment of patients whose mental life is suffused with regret is, in essence, no different from that of patients with other types of problems. The "trio of guideposts" (Pine, 1997), that is, neutrality, abstinence, and anonymity on the analyst's part, and abiding to the "fundamental rule" (Freud, 1900a) of free association on the patient's part, form the structure of the treatment just as they do in other circumstances. At the same time, some specific guidelines can be offered in dealing with cases where regret is chronic and occupies considerable space within the clinical dyad.

First, the analyst must make gentle remarks that validate the patient's regretful stance. For example, if a middle-aged business executive laments his failure to attend his son's college graduation or his nephew's wedding owing to work-related commitments, the analyst must "agree" that such decisions were unfortunate and have resulted in wistful despair. Doing so does not fixate the patient in his *mea culpa* but paves the way for the exploration of why such "bad" decisions were taken in the first place. At the same time, the analyst must be willing to acknowledge that some losses will never be recouped and the passage of time does preclude the possibility of undoing the related damages to the patient's self.

Second, the analyst must help the patient bring forth the changes in his ego ideal that have taken place over the course of time. Clearly, when he took this or that "bad" decision, he was aspiring to be someone other than what he is aspiring to be now. Regret represents not having lived up to one's wished-for self-image and this image during the wistful hand wringing is different from when the decision was taken to do (or not do) what is now regretted. What led to the change? Encouraging the patient to reflect upon this question can yield therapeutically useful information.

Third, the analyst and the patient must be able to observe and discern the "screen" functions of the overt sources of regret. That crying over the impetuousness of adult life helps disavow the impulsivity born out of childhood hunger has to be brought out in the open. For instance, the man who did not attend his son's graduation must come to see that his neglect is a replication of his father's abdication of his paternal responsibilities which, in turn, had acquired an even greater significance for him because of his mother not loving him enough. In other words, the multi-layered roots of contemporary concerns must be unmasked and made subject to mourning. In the course of such unearthing, one might come across "screen memories" (Freud, 1899a) which, to wit, pertain to regret and yet are themselves containers of even earlier dysphoria. No better illustration of this can be given than is embodied in the following reminiscence of the protagonist in J. M. Coetzee's (1998) novel, *Boyhood*.

> He is sitting beside his mother in a bus. It must be cold, for he is wearing red woollen leggings and a woollen cap with a bobble. The engine of the bus labours; they are ascending the wild and desolate Swartberg Pass.
>
> In his hand is a sweet-wrapper. He holds the wrapper out of the window, which is open a crack. It flaps and trembles in the wind.
>
> "Shall I let it go?" he asks his mother.
>
> She nods. He lets it go.
>
> The scrap of paper flies up into the sky. Below there is nothing but the grim abyss of the pass, ringed with cold mountain-peaks. Craning backwards, he catches a last glimpse of the paper, still flying bravely.
>
> "What will happen to it?" he asks his mother, but she does not comprehend.
>
> He thinks all the time of the scrap of paper, alone in all that vastness, that he abandoned when he should not have abandoned it. One day he must go back to the Swartberg Pass and find it and rescue it. That is his duty: he may not die until he has done it. (pp. 30–31)

At first, this passage makes the reader feel that the boy is full of regret at letting the candy wrapper go. Upon giving the matter some thought, however, one notices the inattentiveness of the mother (e.g., her lack of curiosity about the boy's first question and her non-responsiveness to his second question) which might be the real cause of the boy's distress. The lost candy wrapper serves as a screen for the breach in his communication with his mother.

Fourth, the masochistic dimension of regret must be addressed. In commenting upon my paper on "if only …" fantasies, Arnold Cooper noted.

> Those with ferocious superegos and masochistic inclinations are involved in endless self-condemnation: "If only I had said this, if only I had done that" etc. These fantasies have a way of paying

back one's conscience without really intending to do anything different in the future. They are mea culpas …: "I have confessed to
being guilty. And now we can close the book of this episode." (cited
in Akhtar, 1999b, p. 222)

The unconscious masochistic pleasure and the concomitant induction
of helplessness in the analyst that is central to such developments in the
clinical process must be unmasked. The defensive aims of regret against
the emergence of remorse also need to be kept in mind: to carry on endlessly about how one has hurt oneself can preclude acknowledging that
one has hurt others as well due to this or that decision.

Fifth, it should be remembered that a patient's repeated incantations
of regret over a past inaction can serve as a defense against ongoing
procrastination and unwillingness to take on hard work.

Sixth, even during the time when such work is in progress, the analyst must remain respectful of the patient's psychic "soft spots" and be
prepared to oscillate between credulous listening with affirmative intervention (when thwarted growth needs and ego deficits seem to dictate
the transference demands) and sceptical listening with interpretive
intervention (when conflict-based transferences are in the forefront).

Finally, throughout this work, the analyst must remain highly
vigilant towards his own emotional experience. He must avoid a quick
unmasking of the patient's material due to his own restlessness and
exasperation. He must resist the "compulsion to interpret" (Epstein,
1979) and exercise patience both as an attitudinal element and as therapeutic intervention (Akhtar, 2015a). Neither cynicism nor masochistic
submission are permissible to the analyst though their allure is great
while working with such patients.

The guidelines outlined above should not be turned into a rigid
strategy. Maintaining a firm allegiance to the "principle of multiple
function" (Waelder, 1936) in accordance with the patient's material
would help the analyst develop an optimally responsive technique
which fluctuates between "evenly suspended attention" (Freud, 1912e)
and interventions based upon a therapeutic strategy.

Concluding remarks

In this contribution, I have elucidated the phenomenological components of regret and distinguished this particular emotion from the

related one of remorse. I have noted that regret is often accompanied by compromised ego functioning, a ferocious superego, masochism, and the "if only ..." fantasy. I have traced the origins of regret to early breaches in the mother–child relationship and underscored the "screen" functions of the contemporary trauma evoked as a cause of wistfulness by regretful individuals. After a brief foray into literary and sociopolitical realms, I have devoted a section of my discourse to the technical implications of the psychoanalytic understanding of regret.

Now, as I approach the end of this contribution, there are three other areas I wish to comment upon. The first pertains to "survivor's guilt," that is, the feeling of guilt at having been more fortunate than an impaired sibling or having survived while a loved one died in an accident, natural disaster, or a concentration camp (Niederland, 1968). Often the individual who died had been the recipient of guilt-expiating activity; there was unconscious hostility towards him, and his death precluded the possibility of diminishing this guilt by kindness and indulgence towards him (Sonnenberg, 1972). These formulations are impressive but conflate guilt (at the unconscious hostile intentions towards the deceased), remorse (at having "killed" the person via the omnipotence of primary process thinking), and regret (at having done or not done something to protect oneself from the consequences of one's hostility). This link between guilt, remorse, and regret has not been clarified in the existing literature on the topic.

The second area I wish to comment upon is the relationship between regret and suicide. Regret, in tandem with remorse or acting independently, can lead to self-flagellation and diminished self-esteem. When affixed upon actual "misdeeds" and poorly executed decisions of adult life, the emotion of regret can become the *leitmotif* of one's existence. Klein's (1935) suggestion that some suicides represent an individual's effort to rid his love objects of some aspect of himself (e.g., greedy, inconsolable) provides a link between remorse, regret, and suicide. More forceful than this is Winnicott's (1960b) declaration that, at times, suicide is "the destruction of total self in avoidance of annihilation of the true self" (p. 143). This statement suggests that suicide can be a way to thwart a life that seems destined to be replete without authenticity, wistfulness, sorrow, and regret.

The third and last issue I want to touch upon pertains to the self-reform and redemption that can be mobilized by regret. The gnawing awareness of having taken a wrong turn in life or of having missed important opportunities can, sometimes, lead to contemplative self-scrutiny and character transformation. To be sure, some losses cannot be made up (e.g., becoming pregnant in old age) but can be reversed. A high school dropout can pass a GED test and resume education, an immigrant can go back to the country of his origin, an alcoholic who has ruined his physical and financial status can improve on both these fronts. Indeed, substance abuse treatment programs regard the feeling of regret as an ally in the process of recovery. Landman's (1993) assertion that "Regret stimulates thoughts and failings that form a bridge between a regretted past and a better, free future" (p. 23) comes to mind in this context. Kavaler-Adler's (2004) observation that "When regret is conscious it can be grieved on an affective level and learned from on a cognitive level" (p. 75) is also pertinent in this context. A parallel can be found in processes leading to a healthy outcome of remorse. Under fortunate circumstances, meaningful reparation can arise from remorse (Klein, 1935, 1940) and beneficial self-redemption can grow out of regret. No emotion is inherently "good" or "bad" and such qualifiers must be reserved for what one does with a particular emotion's pressure. This applies to all emotions. Regret is no exception.

CHAPTER SIX

Hopelessness

All individuals who seek psychotherapy or psychoanalysis do so because they harbor the hope of sorting things out, improving their lives, and overcoming this or that problem. The extent, intensity, and tenor of the sentiment might vary but the fact that hope is what drives them to seek treatment remains certain. This hope can be realistic (e.g., of becoming able to mourn early losses and availing themselves of what current life does offer in the form of possibilities and gratifications), or pathological (e.g., of reversing time, growing up all over again, bringing dead people alive). And, this hope can be conscious (e.g., of actualizing one's wishes) or unconscious (e.g., of finding development-facilitating objects). It is, therefore, of profound importance to empathize with, discern, uphold, and, at some point, interpretively handle (if necessary) the hope that has brought the patient to the therapist's threshold. The same applies to the pallor or absence of hope. In other words, hope and hopelessness warrant comparable interest from the analyst: recognition, curiosity, exploration, validation, reconstruction, and interpretive resolution. Both poles of this spectrum—hope and hopelessness—are of pertinence to our work. Yet, outside of general psychiatric practice, these issues have received scant attention.

In this chapter, I aim to fill this lacuna. I will begin my discourse with bringing together the scattered psychoanalytic literature on hope and add some of my own views to it. Then I will survey the psychoanalytic literature on the experience of hopelessness and provide a fresh perspective from my own side. I will challenge the reflexive tendency to regard hope as healthy and hopelessness as morbid, demonstrating that both hope and hopelessness have adaptive and pathological variants. I will then delineate the technical implications of the foregoing conceptualizations and conclude with some observations regarding populations that are especially vulnerable to hopelessness and also regarding the existential despair that is the inevitable legacy of our tragically violent world.

Normal and pathological hope

There is a long-held tendency in psychoanalysis to regard optimism in exceedingly positive terms. This tendency was set into motion by Freud's (1917b) well-known correlation of "confidence in success" with being mother's "undisputed darling" (p. 156) and by Abraham's (1924b) linking "imperturbable optimism" (p. 399) with an overly gratifying oral phase. Glover (1925) repeated that profound oral gratification leads to an "excess of optimism which is not lessened by reality experience" (p. 136). Benedek's (1938) upbeat notion of "confident expectation" and Erikson's (1950) normative concept of "basic trust" were similarly anchored in satisfactory outcomes of the infantile-appeal cycle, that is, the infant's expression of need—his gratification by the mother—the infant's return to quiescence. Other contributors (French, 1945; French & Wheeler, 1963; Menninger, 1959) also focused on the positive aspects of hope and optimism.

This positive emphasis on hope found a novel twist in Winnicott's (1956) seminal paper, titled "The antisocial tendency." Winnicott observed that hope, even when expressed through pathological behavior, is essentially healthy and adaptive. He declared that "The antisocial act is an expression of hope" (p. 309) insofar as it seeks redress to an early environmental deprivation. The individual, by behaving in a provocative manner, forces the environment to attend to him. Viewed in this manner, the antisocial tendency is a desperate manifestation of the hope that someone will listen and do something to change the situation. Winnicott went on to state that stealing and destructiveness are always present in the antisocial tendency, though one or the other might be more marked in a given case.

> By *one* trend the child is looking for something, somewhere, and failing to find it seeks elsewhere, when hopeful. By the *other* the child is seeking that amount of environmental stability which will stand the strain resulting from impulsive behavior. This is a search for an environmental provision that has been lost. (p. 310, italics in the original)

The individual who steals is not looking for the stolen object but is seeking a person over whom he could have such unlimited rights. Similarly, destructiveness towards someone is coupled with the hope of being accepted by that person. This "nuisance value" (p. 311) is an essential aspect of the antisocial tendency that seeks repeatedly to test the environment's containing capacity and resilience.[1]

Khan (1966) extended Winnicott's ideas to certain narcissistic and schizoid individuals who seemed uncannily capable of creating special and exciting experiences for themselves, experiences from which they nonetheless withdrew and which left them basically unchanged. It is as if they had hoped for something but did not find it. Casement (1991) related "unconscious hope" to repetition compulsion through which unconscious conflicts continue to generate attempts at solutions which do not actually work. At the same time, patients do contribute in various ways, and "hopefully" (p. 301), to finding the clinical setting needed by them.

In an exception to the "classical" and British independent positive perspective on hope, Angel (1934) noted that optimism can at times be a defensive development.[2] She described five patients with chronic, unrealistic hope of a magical event (*Wunderglauben*) to improve their lots. She traced the origin of three female patients' undue hopefulness to a denial of their lacking a penis and associated feelings of inferiority. Angel offered a different explanation for undue optimism in two male patients. They had been prematurely and painfully deprived of their infantile omnipotence and were seeking its restoration by a fantasied regressive oneness with their mothers. Their optimism contained the hope of such longings being realized. Angel's conceptualization reflected the phallocentrism of psychoanalytic theorizing of her times. The fact most likely is that the latter dynamic applied to her female patients as well.

Over the sixty years following Angel's significant paper, only a few contributions commented upon the defensive functions of excessive optimism. First, Searles (1977) noted that realistic hope needs to be distinguished from "unconscious-denial-based, unrealistic hopefulness" (p. 484). The former emanates from a successful integration of prior disappointments. The latter results from an "essentially manic repression of loss and despair" (p. 483). In contrast to healthy hopefulness, which is a source of support and gratification for oneself and others, excessive hope serves sadomasochistic aims. Searles outlined two connections between such inordinate hope and sadism:

> First, one of the more formidable ways of being sadistic toward the other person is to engender hope, followed by disappointment, in him over and over. Second, the presenting of a hopeful demeanor under some circumstances can constitute, in itself, a form of sadism toward the other person, for it can be expressing, implicitly and subtly, cruel demands upon him to fulfill the hopes written upon one's face. (p. 485)

Following Searles' contribution, Amati-Mehler and Argentieri (1989) described two cases in which "pathological hope" (p. 300) represented "the last and unique possible tie with the primary object, [which] giving up would mean the definite downfall of illusion and the admission that it is really, truly lost" (p. 302). Likewise, Potamianou (1992) asserted that excessive hope can serve as a character armor that keeps reality at a distance. In normal and neurotic conditions, hope sustains a link with the good object and makes waiting bearable. In borderline conditions, however, hope serves as an expression of the patient's narcissistic self-sufficiency; waiting is made bearable only by recourse to infantile omnipotence. For such individuals, the present has only secondary importance. They can tolerate almost any current suffering in the hope that future rewards will make it all worthwhile. Potamianou emphasized that excessive hope, besides fueling (and being fueled by) narcissism, strengthens and prolongs the hidden masochistic suffering of these individuals.

It is in this context that I described "someday ..." fantasies (Akhtar, 1991b, 1994, 1996). These pertain to the feeling that almost all individuals have that a day will come when most of their problems will be solved and they will be at peace. Under normal circumstances such belief is attached to realistic goals, permits some sense of humor, and sustains ambition. But under pathological circumstances, the "someday ..."

fantasy becomes tenacious, imbued with powerful defensive motives, and a servant of regressive, narcissistic, and masochistic aims. Patients vary greatly in the extent to which they provide details of their hopes from "someday …." Often they feel puzzled, uncomfortable, ashamed, and even angry upon being asked to elaborate on their "someday …." This is especially so if they are asked what would happen *after* "someday …." It is as if "someday …," like God, is not to be questioned. Some patients use metaphors and/or visual images to convey the essence of "someday …," while others remain silent about it. Frequently, the analyst has to fill in the blanks and surmise the nature of their expectations from "someday …." In either case, it is the affective texture of "someday …" that seems its most important feature. Basically, "someday …" refers to a time when one would be completely peaceful and conflict-free. Everything would be available, or nothing would be needed. Motor activity would either be unnecessary or effortless. Even thinking would not be required. There would be no aggression from within or from outside. Needless to say, such a universe is also oblivious to the inconvenient considerations of the incest taboo and the anxieties and compromises consequent upon the oedipal situation.

A complex set of psychodynamic mechanisms helps maintain the structural integrity of "someday …": (i) denial and negation of sectors of reality that challenge it, (ii) splitting-off of those self- and object representations that mobilize conflict and aggression, (iii) a defensively motivated feeling of inauthenticity (Gediman, 1985) in those areas of personality where a healthier, more realistic, compromise formation level of mentality and functioning has been achieved, and (iv) a temporal displacement, from past to future, of a preverbal state of blissful unity with the "all good" mother of the symbiotic phase (Mahler, Pine, & Bergman, 1975). The speculation that this fantasy, at its core, contains a longing for a luxurious (and retrospectively idealized) symbiotic phase gains strength from the inactivity, timelessness, wordlessness, thought-lessness, unexcited bliss, and absence of needs implicit in "someday …." This genetic backdrop is supported by my observation that individuals who tenaciously cling to "someday …" had often been suddenly "dropped" from maternal attention during their second year of life (at times due to major external events, for example, birth of a sibling, prolonged maternal hospitalization). However, other factors including early parent or sibling loss, intense castration anxiety, and problematic oedipal scenarios also play a role in the genesis of the "someday …" fantasy. Boys who were excessively close to their mothers, especially if they also had weak or absent fathers, might continue to believe that "someday …" their oedipal triumph could actually be consummated; Chasseguet-Smirgel's (1984) delineation of "perverse character" is pertinent in this context. Girls who were "dropped" by their mothers and valiantly rescued by their fathers persist in the hope of "someday …" finding an all good mother–father combination in adult life.

Mention also needs to be made of Boris's (1976) contribution which juxtaposed hope with desire, noting the frequently antagonistic relationship that exists between them. Delving deeply into this phenomenological realm, Boris declared the following:

> Desire is sensual; hope is not. Desire arises from the cyclic, appetitive passions of the body; hope appears to arise from preconceptions of how things should be. Desire seeks gratification and surcease—it is kinetic; hope is possessive and potential. Desire likes the here-and-now; the definite, the actual; hope likes the yet-to-be, the changeable, the ambiguous. When thwarted, desire tends to retreat, we call it "regress," to its last best success, while hope goes forward beyond even a lifetime or outwards beyond the confines of probability. Desire, frustrated, gives rise to rage and jealousy; hope—to outrage, and to envy and spite and revenge. When renounced, each, however, gives over to sadness; but desire changes its object while hope changes over to desire. (p. 149)

In sum, the psychoanalytic literature on hope can be grouped into three broad categories emphasizing (i) its normative, healthy aspects whereby hope acts as a restraint against the urgency of desire and, in doing so, undergirds sublimation and effort, (ii) its adaptive role in seeking redress, including that through pathological behavior, of early environmental loss, and (iii) its deployment as a defense against early loss and defective object constancy as well as its covert narcissistic and masochistic aims. The nuanced portrayal that emerges from this is that hope can be normal and manifest through healthy aspirations, exist as a subterranean dynamic in outrageousness, and, at times, serve defensive and pathological functions. Similar complexity is to be found in regard to hopelessness.

Normal and pathological hopelessness

Psychoanalytic literature directly pertaining to hopelessness is truly meager. The word "hopelessness" appears all of two times in the entire corpus of Freud's work (Guttman, R. L. Jones, & Parrish, 1980)[3] and the PEP Web offers only six papers with "hopelessness" in their titles over the 116-year history of psychoanalysis. The reasons for this paucity are unclear. Perhaps the darkness of despair leads the observer to recoil from it. Or, the clinical population with greater and sustained hopelessness ends up with general psychiatrists more often than with psychoanalysts. Or, the encounter with true hopelessness propels adjunct, unusual or even "heroic" interventions that the practitioner is averse to putting down on paper. Regardless of etiology, the lack of psychoanalytic literature on hopelessness appears a significant finding in itself.

That being said, the phenomenon of hopelessness first received attention from Spitz (1946, 1960) and Bowlby (1958, 1960, 1961), who observed infants and their reactions to separation from their mothers. They stressed that infants have attachments to their mothers that are independent of "orality" and physiological needs. Upon separating from their mothers, infants at first protest (e.g., crying loudly, looking eagerly for signs of her return), then display increasing hopelessness and despair, and finally resign to the situation and become unenthusiastic about later attachments. Frequent and long separations from mother (e.g., due to her illness or hospitalization), especially when coupled with unreliable replacements, intensify feelings of hopelessness and turn it into a core feature of personality to which the individual can readily regress under need-frustrating circumstances.

An additional viewpoint to this formulation was provided by Kelman (1945), who declared that a love-deprived child constructs an idealized self that is (in imagination) need-free and/or completely able to meet his own needs by the methods of withdrawal, cleverness, or clinging. Since these maneuvers frequently fail, the individual is riddled with dissatisfaction, depression, feelings of doom, chronic hopelessness, and a sense of psychic deadness. The futile striving to eradicate childhood feelings of defectiveness (such as "I am not loved because something is wrong with me") and achieve a peaceful existence in which the child feels loved results in feelings of utter hopelessness and doom. He feels lost, meaningless, and emotionally dead.

> These patients often complain that they are dead ... [and] ... feel that their relationships are dead. They are limited, rigid and controlled. Although they feel that they can move wherever they please, they still feel completely bounded. They suffer from monotony, boredom, and a feeling of ennui. Each day, each feeling, each

> act seems like the one before and the one after. Nothing changes.
> Everything is static and dead. (Kelman, 1945, p. 432)

Schmale (1964) distinguished between "helplessness" and "hopelessness." The former reflects a loss of ego autonomy due to the inability to receive a desired gratification from an important other person. The latter reflects a loss of ego autonomy due to one's own inability to provide oneself with gratification. With a deep anchor in child developmental observations, Schmale proposed that the affect of helplessness occurs first at the end of the oral phase when there is a dawning awareness of being separate from one's mother. Along with this comes the realization of dependence upon her. Now, if the maternal availability (for provision of ego support, gratification of wishes, meeting of developmental needs) is inconsistent, "confident expectation" (Benedek, 1938) fails to develop and the seeds of vulnerability for helplessness (i.e., being unable to draw on others to help) are sowed.

Schmale went on to state that the affect of hopelessness occurs first during the phallic phase where there is increased awareness of sexual wishes on the one hand and strict incest prohibition on the other. It is the inability, at this stage, to provide gratification to oneself that lays down the groundwork for future experiences of hopelessness. Schmale allowed for thinking that some hopelessness might actually be salutary for personality growth.

> The experiencing of the feelings of hopelessness in relation to unfulfilled aspirations, if not too overwhelming or too quickly defended against, leads to a giving up of fantasied wishes. Such giving up is basic to the acceptance of a more realistic sense of self as well as to a more appropriate and realistic awareness of the object world .... A change in psychic self may be necessary to meet and maintain ego autonomy over the ever-pressing instinctual drives and the bodily and external objects. In order to remain reality-oriented and psychically as well as somatically healthy, such changes in self representation are repeatedly required as man grows, explores, achieves, ages, and declines. (p. 308)[4]

The shift from fantasized perfection and desired gratification of prohibited wishes to reality-oriented self perception and achievable pursuits enunciated by Schmale has unmistakable echoes of Klein's (1935) proposal of the "depressive position" in development. Unlike the earlier "paranoid position" characterized by disowning of aggression, retention of a "purified pleasure ego" (Freud, 1915c), omnipotence, greed, envy, and smug certainty, "depressive position" implies the recognition of one's (real and fantasized) destructiveness towards love objects, humility, cognitive flexibility, sadness, gratitude, and reparative longing. Moreover, the nature of hope also changes with this developmental achievement. In "paranoid position," the hope is one of perfection and purity. In "depressive position," the hope is one of relatedness and love. In Klein's (1957) own words:

> This hope is based on the growing unconscious knowledge that the internal and external object is not as bad as it was felt to be in its split-off aspects. Through mitigation of hatred by love, the object improves in the infant's mind. It is no longer so strongly felt to have been destroyed in the past and the danger of its being destroyed in the future is lessened …. The internal object acquires a restraining and self-preservative attitude. (p. 196)

Thus, in Klein's formulation, real hope emerges only after false (i.e., idealized) hope has been given up and when love predominates over hate in the internal psychic economy of the child. In other words, a certain "normal" hopelessness is essential for psychic growth; the germ of this idea seems inherent in Freud's (1911b) distinction between "pleasure principle" and "reality principle" whereby the hope of gratification, in order to be safe and therefore more satisfying, has to give up its urgency in the moment.

The experience of hopelessness also drew the attention of Miller (1985), and Amati-Mehler and Argentieri (1989). Miller described chronic hopelessness in the setting of pathological narcissism. The narcissistic person cannot experience a feeling of being loved; he derides it as mere "admiration" or based upon others' not knowing him well enough. He cannot love himself either. As a result, he feels perpetually hopeless to connect with others and with his own self. There is also the sense that one can never vent the pent-up rage within oneself since this rage is against the caretakers (past and present) upon whom one feels dependent. Amati-Mehler and Argentieri (1989) emphasized that the way of chronic hopelessness is paired by inward clinging to the pathological hope that "what is past or lost forever can still be provided and restored" (p. 300).

There is no alternative intermediary space between how "it was" and how "it should be"; pathological hope cancels realistic hope and gives way to hopelessness. Real chances available in life are dismissed, or rather not recognized, because they do not fit the rigid mold that illusion pretends to realize. Capacity to feel and experience oneself as occupying a dynamic-spatial-temporal dimension, in relation to others too, enhances difficult symbolic tension to make it possible to think, to discriminate fantasy from reality and personage from person, and thus to organize boundaries of mental representation linked with intrapsychic and interpersonal separation processes. What distinguishes the case we observed instead is a situation in which a very tenuous ridge divides illusion from disillusion: experiences of painful separation cannot be denied nor can they be accepted; there's an eternal present in which loss is furiously felt, but the "drama" which *has already irreparably happened* is not recognized or realized as such. (p. 300, italics in the original)

Putting all the foregoing material together, I can envision five vertices to conceptualize the experience of hopelessness. These include the following.

- *Normal versus pathological hopelessness*, with the former emanating from the renunciation of infantile omnipotence and aiding personality development, and the latter clinging to that very omnipotence and fueling fixation on unrealistic goals.
- *Focal versus generalized hopelessness*, with the former pertaining to the dawning sense that certain specific aims will not be realized and the latter to not finding any aspect of life gratifying and meaningful.
- *Situational versus characterological hopelessness*, with the former ensuing largely from contemporary environmental barriers to gratification and the latter emanating from the internalization of an early, severely disappointing, environment.
- *Melancholic versus militant hopelessness*, with the former expressing a wish to give up on this world out of a sense of existential fatigue, and the latter representing a relentless attack upon others with the knife of loud despair.
- *Pleading versus resistant hopelessness*, with the former serving as a desperate method to pull the caretaker close so as to receive love and attention and the latter to render the caretaker helpless by keeping

him away from the horrible infantile trauma that is being repudiated by the preoccupation with the present moment.

Such conceptualization prepares us to consider the technical measures needed to help patients with the anguish of pathological hope and pathological hopelessness.

Technical implications

From the foregoing discourse, it is clear that pathological hope is a defense against the unbearable experience of hopelessness. The individual who tenaciously clings to inordinate optimism (regardless of whether it is manifested through fierce ambition, flailing search, or futile waiting) is, at his psychic base, unable and unwilling to accept the devastating loss of love and support experienced during childhood. He cannot bear hopelessness that lurks just below the surface of his excessive hope. This dynamic becomes evident gradually as the treatment proceeds. More striking is the converse of it, that is, the slow unearthing of pathological hope under the manifest surface of intense hopelessness. Individuals who insistently and constantly declare themselves to be hopeless turn out to be harboring (however secretly) manic expectations of total reversal of their childhood trauma. Considered this way, pathological hope and pathological hopelessness appear to be twins: maladaptive responses to the inability to tolerate normal hopelessness and sustain normal hope. Both pathological hope and pathological hopelessness are seen in the setting of severe childhood frustrations, even though the patients tend to repeat rather than recall the (actual and fantasized) relational scenarios consequent upon such trauma.

Treatment of these individuals must rest upon the general principles of handling psychic trauma outlined in psychoanalytic literature as well as upon certain specific interventions vis-à-vis pathological hope and hopelessness. Surveying the literature on the former aspect, I have recently (Akhtar, 2014b) delineated the following twelve features of technique.

Welcoming attitude

A genuinely warm attitude on the analyst's part must be discernible by the patient. He or she must come to feel that the analyst is happy to be doing this work and that he welcomes the patient to his office and, behind that, to his inner world. Leo Stone (1981) stated that "The 'love' implicit in empathy, listening, and trying to understand, in non-seductive devotion to the task, the sense of full acceptance, respect, and sometimes the homely phenomenon of sheer dependable patience, may take their place as equal or nearly equal in importance to sheer interpretive skills" (p. 114). This is nowhere more true than in the course of treating individuals with a history of severe psychic trauma.

Prolonged "holding"

A longer than usual period of waiting for the patient to become "analyzable" is needed in such cases. The patient must be psychologically "held" (Winnicott, 1960a, 1960b) and must not be rushed. He or she must be allowed a sufficient (often, quite long) length of time to experience, at different levels, the soundness of the therapeutic rapport (Amati-Mehler & Argentieri, 1989; Balint, 1968). Premature rupture of the patient's defensiveness and/or withdrawal can traumatize him all over again. Interpretations given while the patient is in need of affirmation and "holding" can cause hurt even if they are content-wise correct.

Flexible framework

The analyst must be able and willing to judiciously accommodate the frame to the patient's post-traumatic idiosyncrasies. For instance, if the patient shows up at the office with a baby or a dog, the analyst should permit it, remain "unobtrusive" (Balint, 1968), and let the process unfold. Patients' irregular attendance for sessions might similarly have to be "tolerated" and quietly understood (i.e., without interpretation) for a long time (Gerrard, 2011). This does not allow outrageous concessions to reality nor does it preclude skeptical thinking about such actions. However, patience, affirmation, and accommodation should be given premium over unmasking and deciphering for a reasonably long time after beginning the treatment.

Validation of trauma

Nanette Auerhahn and Dori Laub's (1987) concept of "joint acceptance of the reality of the Holocaust," requiring the analyst to demonstrate his acknowledgement of the factual nature of this great tragedy, applies to all severe trauma. The analyst dealing with such situations must validate that the event or events (e.g., sexual abuse by a parent, death of a parent in early childhood, physical brutality) have indeed been horrible things that the patient has had to bear. Of course, if the patient gets "hooked" on repeatedly wanting to hear this from the analyst, the matter has to be dealt with in an interpretive manner. But validation of the psychic impact of trauma must always be the first step.

Belief in the principle of multiple function

The analyst must subscribe to the "principle of multiple function" (Waelder, 1936) and realize that any phenomenon the patient presents is multi-layered and but one part of the overall gestalt of his or her psyche. Otherwise, the desperate monotony and/or violent simplicity of the patient's overt material (and its transference implications) can tempt the analyst into symptom-based and directly ameliorative interventions. Conviction that each psychological matter has many determinants and many purposes allows the analyst's work-ego the much needed latitude. Thus armed, the analyst can accommodate various perspectives on the patient's psychopathology including oedipal vs. preodipal (Greenspan, 1977), defense vs. discharge (Arlow & Brenner, 1964), romantic vs. classical (Strenger, 1989), conflict vs. deficit (Killingmo, 1989), etc. Oscillations between these contradictory perspectives would prevent the analyst from succumbing to simplistic and uni-factorial explanations of the patient's psychopathology.

Sensitivity to nonverbal communications

In treating severely traumatized individuals, the analyst has to be sharply attuned to their nonverbal communications. Such patients often behave rather than remember and report. Fantasy elaboration is meager and "The raw data pointing to interruptions early in ego development tend to be affectual rather than verbal or intellectual" (Burland, 1975, p. 317). The "unrememberable and the unforgettable" (A. Frank, 1969) residues of trauma, however, lie unabated under the adult persona and are often discernible only through the patient's posture and movements on the couch, mannerisms, tone of voice, and style of entering and leaving the office. Paying attention to such "behavioral dance and somatic music" (McLaughlin, 1992, p. 151) opens new vistas for reconstruction and insight.

Enhancement of verbalization

Psychic trauma interferes not only with the consolidation of self-and-object constancy but also with the ego's capacity to recognize and regulate inner affective states. The analyst therefore has to become an auxiliary ego for the patient in this regard, introducing him or her to the feeling states that are active in a given moment. Annie Katan (1961) made this point when she said that "Verbalization leads to an increase of the controlling function of the ego over affects and drives" (p. 185). Comments like "You are very angry right now," "What you are experiencing is extremely painful," and "You seem very, very sad," while appearing mundane, go a long way in helping the patient's ego achieve ascendency over the inner chaos and organize the material in a way that later becomes amenable for more conventional interpretive handling.

Creation of transitional space

A related matter is that of creating psychic space in which the seed of deep analytic process might be sowed. Traumatized individuals are often bifurcated and unable to bear ambivalence. "Your way or my way," "Now or never," "All or nothing," "Love or hate," constitute the furniture of their psychic living rooms (Lewin & Schulz, 1992). To mend such splits, the analyst has to make "bridging interventions" (Kernberg, 1975), that is, comments that display, by gentle verbal reminders or a subtle shift in the tone of voice, that he has not "forgotten" the transference configuration that is opposite to the one currently active. More important than this, the analyst has to pry open the closed (or, create the hitherto nonexistent) "transitional space" (Winnicott, 1953) for the patient and enhance the capacity for "mentalization" (Fonagy & Target, 1997). For instance, if the patient habitually concludes his or her thoughts by saying, "I have nothing more to say about this," the analyst might suggest that the patient try saying it in a slightly different manner, as "I have nothing more *that I know* to say about this." This, as it is clear, would open up new possibilities for topographically layered material to emerge. Or, if the patient says (for instance, in response to a wish to have sex with the analyst) that "Look, I know you will say 'No' to it," the analyst might say, "What if I did not say 'No'?" And then, upon the patient's panicky response: "You are scaring me now. Are you saying 'Yes'?" the analyst might respond by a "No" again, pointing out to the patient, "Let us talk about it" as a possible response that avoids a "Yes-No" answer. And so on. The point is to impel the patient to think afresh by demonstrating fresh thinking on one's own part.

Attunement to patients' fluctuating psychostructural organization

Once the analysis really gets going, the analyst must be able to fluctuate between the two poles of "credulous listening leading to affirmative interventions" and "skeptical listening leading to interpretive interventions." Putting aside the superego-fear of "not interpreting" and the id-greed of "always interpreting," the analyst must operate from his ego and its deep contact with the patient's fluctuating psychic organization. When the patient shifts from ordinary conflict-based transferences and moves into the traumatized sector of the self and object representations,

> … the investigative attitude no longer matches the structural level of the patient and the analyst has to change his strategy. If not, his intervention is likely to act as an assault against the self representation of the patient …. It should also be remembered that the quality of the transference may be closed to the structural turning point and so is apt to change rapidly. According, the analyst should be in a state of constant receptivity for oscillation between the two strategic positions. (Killingmo, 1989, p. 74)

Utilization of developmental interventions

The analyst working with traumatized individuals must also keep in mind the dialectical relationship between the interpretive resolution of psychopathology and the resumption of arrested development (Settlage, 1993). With each undoing of post-traumatic pathology, there is the opportunity for resumed development in that area and with each such developmental advance there is an increase in the patient's tolerance for the exposure of sequestered anxiety-producing memories, wishes, and fantasies. Samuel Abrams's (1978) "developmental intervention" becomes a specific tool in this regard. When a hitherto unexpressed healthy tendency emerges as a result of ongoing clinical work, the analyst must not interpretively deconstruct it; instead, he should underscore the inherent progressive trend in it and "facilitate the emergence of experiential building blocks" (p. 397). Calvin Settlage's (1993) recommendation that the analyst acknowledge and encourage the patient's developmental initiatives and achievements belongs in the same realm.

Facilitation of mourning

The analyst has to recognize that mourning-like elements, integral to analyses, carry greater significance in the treatment of traumatized patients. Such individuals have not gone through the incremental steps of loss (of external support and of omnipotence) and gain (of internal structure and of reality principle) typical of the gradual maturation of personality. They lack this prototype of mourning. Separations from the analyst, guilty recognition of their aggression towards him, dawning gratitude, and the renewed anguish of loss during termination—all awaken and consolidate the process of mourning. The same applies to the loss of their infantile omnipotence and their frequent tendency to live in a world of illusions. The latter proclivity is especially evident in the addiction to revenge-seeking (in reality or fantasy) or, conversely, in the near-manic hope that one day all wounds will be healed, all grievances heard, and all cruelties by others apologized for and forgiven. Arriving at a realization that this might not be so and the sadness that accompanies such a realization is an integral part of the treatment of traumatized individuals.

Management of countertransference

Traumatized patients bring to us horrifying tales of abuse, heart-wrenching wails of desperation, the burden of futility, and the scarring daggers of revenge-seeking. All this can create a countertransference havoc. This has to be borne and diligently used as a source of information, even during (or soon after) the moments when his "role responsiveness" (Sandler, 1976) forces him into a mutual enactment with the patient. It should be remembered that "The analyst's emotional response to his patient within the analytic situation represents one of the most important tools of his work—it is an instrument of research into the patient's unconscious" (Heimann, 1950, p. 81). Elsewhere, I have delineated (Akhtar, 2013b) how the analyst's listening to his own associations, impulses, affects, and actions—both deliberate and inadvertent—informs him about the deeper undercurrents of the process unfolding within the clinical dyad. While true for all clinical work, such vigilance is of greater importance in working with traumatized individuals.

In addition to work along the guidelines mentioned above, such patients require certain specific interventions. For instance, after establishing an atmosphere of trust and security and after ample use of "affirmative interventions" (Killingmo, 1989)[5], the analyst must help the patient unmask what underlies his waiting attitude. This will pave the way for the two of them to squarely face the idealization inherent in "someday ..." fantasies. For instance, to a patient who, after four years of analytic work, continued to complain bitterly about the ineffectiveness of psychoanalysis vis-à-vis his short stature (a disguised but closed version of his actual complaint), I once responded by saying, "You know, the pained disbelief in your voice and the intensity with which you berate me about this issue makes me wonder if you really believe that analysis could or should lead you to become taller. Do you?" The patient was taken aback but, after some hesitation, did acknowledge that all along he had believed that he might become taller as a result of our work. Similarly, to a patient who constantly wept and expressed profound hopelessness, I said, "What exactly are you hopeless about?" And, on another occasion, I said, "If you are too certain that nothing will come out of this treatment, how are we to understand your coming so regularly and for such a long time for your sessions?" In both instances, the patient's initial reaction was to brush my questions aside but, after further confrontation and questioning, the patient began to see the split-off and unrealistic hope that underlay her vociferous pessimism.

Once such omnipotent expectations from analysis are brought to the surface, the analyst can help the patient bring forth the narcissistic and masochistic gratifications derived from these fantasies, which keep the patient's existence in a grand, suffering limbo. He might now point out to the patient the illusory nature of his "someday ..." fantasy. However, even during this phase, the analyst must remain respectful of the patient's psychic "soft spots" and be affectively and conceptually prepared to oscillate between affirmative interventions, when thwarted growth needs and ego deficits seem to dictate the transference demands, and interpretive interventions, when more traditional conflict-based transference is in the forefront. Such "oscillations in strategy" (Killingmo, 1989, p. 75) would necessitate a conceptual freedom on the analyst's part to view the patient's idealization as both a thwarted developmental need and a pathological defense—that is, a psychic configuration requiring both empathic and interpretive handling.

Failing to engage the patient in such an interpretive undertaking, the analyst must be prepared to rupture the patient's inordinate hope. Clearly, many analysts would question the need ever to rupture the patient's excessive hope. They would suggest that simply understanding its origins and functions and letting the usual analytic approach take its course would lead to the transformation of such fantasies. This does happen in milder cases. However, in those stubbornly fixated on "someday ..." fantasies, it comes down to "having to state that neither analysis nor analyst [is an] omnipotent rescuer, as the patients in their illusion needed to believe" (Amati-Mehler & Argentieri, 1989, p. 301). With those endlessly lamenting a long-dead parent, the analyst might have to literally confirm the irreversibility of the situation. A less dramatic, but essentially similar, example is of the patient who "kept crying and saying, 'I can't help it,' and the analyst [who] said: 'I am afraid I can't help it either'" (Amati-Mehler & Argentieri, 1989, p. 296).

Such interventions can be subsumed under the broad rubric of "optimal disillusionment" (Gedo & Goldberg, 1973), which requires that the analysand learn to give up magical thinking. They are neither conventional nor risk-free. They disrupt the transference dynamics and can be traumatic to the patient. Indeed, when their "dosage" or timing is inappropriate—and this may not be entirely predictable—the resulting despair and psychic pain might lead the patient to become seriously suicidal. This puts the analysis to a most severe test. Temporary departures from neutrality might now become unavoidable and adjunct, stabilizing measures might have to be deployed. On the other hand, interventions of this sort might constitute a turning point of the analytic process in less complicated circumstances, provided, of course, the analyst's "holding functions" are in place, and the effects of such an intervention can be analyzed. Rupture of pathological hope is a necessary precondition for mourning that is otherwise blocked in these patients. At the same time, the analyst:

> Must convey to the patient not only the direction he wants the patient to move in, but also confidence that the movement is inherent in the patient, which means that what the uncured patient wants is indeed a representation, however distorted, of what the cured patient will get. (Friedman, 1969, p. 150)

In other words, the analyst must make sure that the consequence of his intervention is not a transition from pathological hope to hopelessness but one from pathological hope to realistic hope. This movement is facilitated if the analyst has faith in the patient's capacity in this regard, a proposition reflecting Loewald's (1960) outlining of the childhood need to identify with one's growth potential as seen in the eyes of one's parents.

In cases where pathological hopelessness is on the surface, unrealistic hope lurks underneath. According to Miller (1985):

> The depressed patient harbors the secret hope that he will be reunited or merged with the eternal, omnipotent object (to some, death). It is one of the things which he does not say and which he does not let himself become aware of consciously. The expression of hopelessness about himself is a way of expressing this hope indirectly while at the same time keeping it out of conscious awareness. By repetitively expressing hopelessness about himself—his worth, his abilities, his being able to change, etc.—he prevents himself from experiencing the true hopelessness of attaining this state of paradise …. The other crucial aspect of this understanding of depression and of the expression of hopelessness is the way in which is it used in the attack on the object. (p. 75)

In such cases, interventions must focus upon validation of the patient's anguish, reconstruction of the lack of love during childhood, and the masochistic dependence upon the internalized "dead mother" (Green, 1980). If the patient shows a militant quality to hopelessness in the clinical situation and the analyst feels himself to be a target of sadism, then that too has to be interpreted. However, the risk in doing so is to increase the patient's guilt which, in turn, can preclude his internalization of the analyst's kindness and concern. The tetrad of (i) repudiated horror (about how negligent and coldly cruel one's parents were), (ii) the distorted self-assessment of parental "gaslighting" (Barton & Whitehead, 1969), (iii) the hatred consequent upon early deprivation, and (iv) the pervasive guilt over this hatred as well as over one's existence, impedes recognizing, accepting, and assimilating the goodness offered by the analyst. Needless to add that throughout this work, the analyst must be highly vigilant toward his own emotional experience. Within transference, the analyst is invested by these patients with the task of preserving an illusion. This puts pressure on the analyst. On the one hand, there is temptation to actively rescue the patient. On the other hand, there is the allure of quickly showing the patient that his expectations are unrealistic and serve defensive aims. Cloaked in the guise of therapeutic zeal, hasty attempts of this sort often emanate from the analyst's own unresolved narcissism and infantile omnipotence. "The determinedly optimistic therapist coerces ... his patients into experiencing the depression which he is too threatened to feel within himself" (Searles, 1977, p. 483). Clearly, both extremes (rescue and rejection) are to be avoided. In this context, the issue of the analyst's own hope is pertinent (see also Mitchell, 1993).[6] While he does envision an ego more free of conflicts in the patient's future, his hope must not become unrealistic. An analyst-analysand collusion around waiting for an omnipotent solution for the patient's suffering is a certain recipe for an interminable analysis.

Concluding remarks

In this contribution, I have elucidated the developmental foundations of hope and hopelessness. On a phenomenological and psychodynamic level, I have delineated the normal (adaptive and growth-promoting) and pathological (maladaptive and fixation-fueling) variants of both hope and hopelessness. I have emphasized that the experience of both hope and hopelessness (the latter in limited, focal, and phase-appropriate dosages) is necessary for healthy personality development. After laying down such a foundation, I have delineated the technical strategies necessary in the treatment of pathologically optimistic and pathologically hopeless patients.

Now, before closing, I wish to touch upon two other areas. The first pertains to special populations that might be more vulnerable to a sense of hopelessness in life. The second pertains to the avoidance of hopelessness in a world replete with hunger, uneven distribution of resources, oppression, and war. As far as special populations with greater vulnerability to hopelessness is concerned, those afflicted with serious poverty come to mind first along with those who are politically oppressed, socially disenfranchised, and otherwise disadvantaged. Children who grow up in homes where their basic needs could not be met and where a "climate of defeated parents" (Symonds, 1968, p. 16) prevailed often carry profound, even if covert[7] hopelessness in their hearts. The sense of there being no escape from the soul-crushing realities of their environment gets internalized over time and dooms the ego's capacities for hope, patience, and sustained effort. Crowded living arrangements, often associated with poverty, overexpose the child to the vagaries of adult behavior and this, in turn, adds to disillusionment. Severe socio-political oppression, restriction of movement and travel, segregation along racial lines, and apartheid-like governmental policies contribute to feeling helpless and hopeless; those subject to such circumstances find little reason for optimism and become fatalistic.

The effect of old age and infirmity on hope and hopelessness also deserve consideration. To be sure, it is the collective economy of good internal objects that regulates the capacity for optimism in life; nonetheless, the increasing loss of bodily and cognitive functions during old age often erodes this inner confidence. Semel (1990) writes about the prevalence of themes of hopelessness in the treatment of older patients and Lax (2008), in an especially poignant paper titled, "Becoming really old: the indignities," has elucidated the everyday struggle of the elderly to retain hope and not succumb to hopelessness.

> Unconsciously, the loss of any body function is experienced as an irreparable and continuous blow to the self, a partial death for which there is no repair. It is accompanied by a depletion of self-love. No helpful device (a hearing aid, glasses, a cane, an electric wheelchair, etc.) can substitute for the quality of the function that is impaired or that no longer exists. All aids are, at best, "make do." The impaired self-image is experienced as being *inferior, no longer whole*. Fear arises: what will happen next? A partial regression may occur.
>
> Some people react to their aging bodies with a sense of hate and disparagement; some look at themselves with despair and are overwhelmed by a sense of helplessness. They feel that "nothing can be done." Some may even feel guilty and blame themselves for not having done something earlier to prevent their present state, but when asked, "What that could have been?," they fall silent. (p. 842, italics in the original)

Finally, there is the much broader question of how to maintain hope for mankind in a world rife with ethnic conflicts, territorial aggressions, genocides, and the ever-present threat of nuclear Armageddon (Slochower, 1984). Certainly, political praxis, including that which is psychoanalytically informed (Varvin & Volkan, 2005; Volkan, 1999, 2004, 2006), can be of assistance in making the circumstances less dire, and disarmament agreements can reduce the threat to the life on our planet. In the end, however, it is the fierce preservation and celebration of goodness which already exists in this world—in the form of altruism, courage, freedom, democracy, poetry, art, and love—that strengthen our hope and make our hopelessness bearable.

Sorrow and audacity

To bear sorrow gracefully is the right thing to do. At least that's what the British would have us believe. But then, they have the same prescription for all feelings: bear them, with grace. Folks from Finland and Japan have also mastered this art; they don't say a word about sorrow. The Spanish, Portuguese, and Mexicans are different. They do not attempt to bear or bury emotions, including, of course, sorrow. They seek to transform it into song, afternoon sex, poetry, and high-pitched family drama. Indians visit temples, Puerto Ricans cook up a storm, Italians drink their wine, and Germans try engineering and mathematics. Facing the multiplicity of ways to handle sorrow (or, shall we say, of being handled by sorrow), a thinking person—which I self-indulgently declare myself to be and, quickly seeking forgiveness for the immodesty, include you in this category—is compelled to ask what actually is a "good" response to sorrow.

One's cultural background pushes its list of options. One's temperament instinctively prefers a path. And, one's internalized role models exert their own influence. As a result, what might appear as "choice" under such circumstances, often turns out to be a mandate.

The trick then is to shun all the obvious pathways and strive for audacity. Not of the self-harming kind, mind you. Going to a circus,

131

when feeling suffocated by sorrow, is the sort of thing I have in mind. Trust me, seeing a badly dressed midget on a trapeze can heal a lot, even if momentarily. Another remedy might involve walking backwards the entire day for three consecutive Tuesdays. Or, deciding that, come hell or high water, you will drink a full can of orange soda at precisely 11:00 a.m. each day for a week. Get the point? No? All right, let me put on my teacher's hat and explain. See, what I'm trying to convey is akin to Dylan Thomas's advice: "Do not go gentle into that good night." I am advocating an assertion of what has been called the "will to recovery". Sorrow is a big beast that one can hardly defeat with only professional help though that is needed and useful. Some distraction and defiance are also essential to amuse this intimidating monster. And, once you succeed in bringing a smile to its face, the beast will begin to act friendly towards you. The son of a bitch might even bestow upon you the skill of self-scrutiny, the pleasure of good writing, or at least, the art of making a perfect omelette. Who knows?

NOTES

Chapter One

1. See in this regard my paper, "The compulsion to betray and the need to be betrayed" (Akhtar, 2013a), which elaborates upon the problems caused by such gullibility.
2. I have elsewhere (Akhtar, 2003) described the characteristics of a good mentor and noted the overlaps and distinctions such a role has with those of a parent, a teacher, a lover, and a psychotherapist.
3. See Akhtar (2011, pp. 87–122) for a comprehensive review of psycho-analytic literature on this topic.
4. Shneidman asserted that the dying individual can imagine and influence how he will be and wants to be remembered after he is gone. He called this posthumous, self-created image "post-self."
5. Sanguinetti (2016) has recently explicated the relationship between different forms of government and public trust.
6. A friend of mine, Rachana Maitra, recently told me that her father, editor of the Indian newspaper, *Statesman*, Sri Niranjan Majumder (1920–1975) had, at the age of eighteen, dispatched a poem in response to this poem by Tagore. The great poet wrote back: "I like the poem you have written in response to my poem, 'Question'. It is worthy of publication"

(letter dated August 24, 1938; shared with me in a personal communication by Ms. Maitra on January 14, 2016).

Chapter Two

1. The current nosological system of psychiatry (DSM-V, 2013) mentions jealousy in two contexts: delusional disorder—jealous type—and obsessive jealousy. The former refers to an encapsulated delusion of infidelity without auditory hallucinations and other grossly disorganizing features of psychosis. The latter refers to a "non-delusional preoccupation with a partner's perceived infidelity" (p. 139). The assignment of the latter category to the broad group of obsessive compulsive disorder is questionable in my mind. The non-psychotic jealous person does not experience his suspicions as ego-dystonic. In fact, he is inclined to regard such doubts as plausible. He draws considerable masochistic gratification from them. Moreover, while the true obsessional who obtains temporary relief upon being told that what he fears shall not come true, the jealous person bristles at such reassurance and begins to pile up more evidence to prove himself right.
2. In bestowing such importance upon the role of sibling relationship in personality development, Klein was noticeably ahead of her times.
3. Elsewhere, I have elucidated the role of lightheartedness in the capacity for being playful (Akhtar, 2011, pp. 65–84).
4. The intimacy and precision of Wisdom's (1976) description makes one wonder if the boy in question was actually his own child. If true, this will not be the first instance of such a sort in psychoanalytic literature. Many analysts, beginning with Freud (1920g), have used observations regarding their children or grandchildren to make a theoretical point.
5. For a detailed explication of the role inanimate objects play in human mental life, see Akhtar (2003, 2005).
6. This list is restricted to high-quality films and does not refer to the mediocre (and simply bad) movies that are the daily staple of TV channels like Lifetime Movies.
7. While a systems-based approach to jealousy, especially in the setting of marital therapy, might be useful in certain situations, I do not have experience in couples work and suggest that the interested reader look up pertinent literature from this sub-specialty (especially S. Friedman, 1989; Guerin, Fay, Burden, & Kautto, 1987; Pam & Pearson, 1994).
8. Klein (1928), however, believed that "Jealousy plays a greater part in women's lives than in men's, because it is reinforced by deflected envy of the

mate on account of the penis" (p. 195). She also held that women possess a greater capacity for disregarding their own wishes and for sacrifice. Putting these two observations together, Klein concluded that women are capable of emotions that range from "the most petty jealousy to the most self-forgetful loving-kindness" (p. 195).

Chapter Three

1. In opening this section with Bergmann, I am not overlooking that long before him, Balint (1948) had made significant contributions to the psychoanalytic understanding of love. I am reserving comments on Balint's work for a later section of the paper where his ideas fit better.
2. In a reflexive derision of such "arranged marriages, public opinion in the West tends to overlook that marriages based on self-selection and love frequently fall apart. The rate of divorce in the United States is especially appalling" (Akhtar & Blue, 2017).
3. Haynal's (1988, 2002) explication of the Germanic-Hungarian cultural influences upon Freud and Ferenczi, respectively, is instructive in this context. Haynal notes Ferenczi to have possessed "a very Budapest brand of mischievousness" (2002, p. 53) which, in part, affected his technique.

Chapter Four

1. Extending this observation to the malady of a "shy narcissist," I have noted (2000) that such a person feels "especially uncomfortable upon being photographed; the attention of a camera suddenly floods his ego with primitive exhibitionism and causes him much anxiety" (p. 115).
2. With characteristic misogyny, Freud (1905d) went on to compare such proclivity on the child's part with the disposition of "an average uncultured woman" (p. 191).
3. Such "unshame" can also be found in the setting of functional psychoses, advanced dementia, and traumatic injuries involving the frontal region of the brain.
4. For an elucidation of this elusive concept, see Akhtar, 2015b.
5. Wurmser (1981), who coined the terms "theatophilia" and "delophilia," described them as follows. Theatophilia referred to "the desire to watch and observe, to admire and to be fascinated, to merge and master through attentive looking, operating as a basic inborn drive from earliest infancy" (p. 158). Delophilia stood for "the desire to express oneself and

to fascinate others by one's self-exposure, to show and to impress, to merge with the other through communication. Again, it would originate in archaic times" (p. 158).

6. Though not naming it as such, I have elsewhere (Akhtar, 2011) described "the shame of the motherless child" in connection with the lifelong impact of early maternal loss.

7. "Such internal pressures are not exclusive in their capacity to override the shame barrier. Dire economic conditions and abject poverty can also drive one to behaviors that would otherwise be considered 'shameless'. An encounter with beggars in poor countries demonstrates this dynamic poignantly" (Priti Shukla, personal communication, May 28, 2015).

8. Shameless candor as a character trait was strikingly evident in the ex-marine officer, Jeffrey McDonald, who murdered his wife and children in cold blood (McGinniss, 1983).

9. The sporty practice of "skinny dipping" and the ever-so-slightly intimidating nude beaches and nudist colonies bring out the shame-shamelessness tension within one and the same culture.

10. A young Iranian psychoanalytic candidate once said to me: "I will die of shame if I have to say the words for sex and genitals in Persian to a patient" (personal communication, April, 11, 2001, name withheld upon request). I smiled and encouraged her to explore this issue further on her own as well as in her analysis. I also reassured her that she was not alone in experiencing such anxieties, adding that even Freud lapsed into the Latin *matrem nudam* while describing, at age forty-one, the childhood memory of having seen his mother naked (letter to Fliess, October 3, 1897, cited in Masson, 1985, p. 268).

Chapter Five

1. I have elsewhere (Akhtar, 1996) elucidated the link between nostalgia and optimism in greater detail. There I have demonstrated the essential similarity between the "if only ..." and "someday ..." fantasies.

2. For further references of this sort, and for the place of regret in the culture at large, see the magisterial work of Janet Landman, 1993.

3. Another good example of such "warm regret" is to be found in the 1957 Bollywood film song, "*Sub kuchh luta ke hosh mein aaye to kya kiya,*" which means "After having squandered everything, what good is it that I am wise now!"

Chapter Six

1. Winnicott (1960a, 1963) reiterated this conceptualization a number of times and it seems to undergird his technical approach to patients in general.
2. Nearly two hundred years before this, Voltaire (1759) had declared optimism to be "a mania for maintaining that all is well when things are going badly" (p. 54).
3. This is striking in the light of a deep pessimistic bent to Freud's view of mankind, the "strange feelings of inferiority" (E. Jones, 1955, p. 3) he suffered from, his "punishing conscience" (Gay, 1988, p. 140), and his remarkable insights (Freud, 1917e) into the problem of melancholia.
4. Freud's (1914c) statement regarding the importance of retaining the capacity for love speaks to the same point. He said, "A strong egoism is a protection against falling ill, but in the last resort we must begin to love in order to not fall ill, and we are bound to fall ill if, in consequence of frustration, we are unable to love" (p. 85).
5. Such interventions are composed of an "objectifying element," which conveys the sense to the patient that the therapist can feel what it is to be in the former's shoes, a "justifying element," which introduces a cause-and-effect relationship, and an "accepting element," which imparts a historical context to the current distress by including the mention of similar experiences from the patient's childhood. Affirmative interventions often necessitate that the analyst deliberately restrict the scope of his communication, yet such superficiality paradoxically prepares the ground for unmasking interpretive interventions.
6. The question of the analyst's hope remains open with some analysts (Bion, 1967; Boris, 1976) suggesting that he approach the patient without preconceived aspirations and other analysts (Hoffman, 1992; Loewald, 1960) advocating the importance of analysts' optimism for the progress of treatment.
7. The occasional hedonism of their adult lifestyle during adulthood reflects what Boris (1976) has described as the "fundamental antagonism between hope and demise" (p. 141); possession of hope acts as a restraint against desire and loss of hope results in a burgeoning of desire.

REFERENCES

Abraham, K. (1924a). The influence of oral eroticism on character formation. In: *Selected Papers of Karl Abraham, M. D.* (pp. 393–406). New York: Brunner/Mazel, 1955.

Abraham, K. (1924b). A short study of the development of the libido, viewed in the light of mental disorders. In: *Selected Papers on Psychoanalysis* (pp. 418–501). New York: Brunner/Mazel, 1955.

Abrams, S. (1978). The teaching and learning of psychoanalytic developmental psychology. *Journal of the American Psychoanalytic Association, 26*: 387–406.

Affair to Remember, An (1957). Directed by L. McCarey. Twentieth Century Fox production.

Akhtar, S. (1984). The syndrome of identity diffusion. *American Journal of Psychiatry, 141*: 1381–1385.

Akhtar, S. (1985). *The Hidden Knot.* Chicago, IL: Adams Press.

Akhtar, S. (1990). Paranoid personality disorder: a synthesis of developmental, dynamic, and descriptive features. *American Journal of Psychotherapy, 44*: 5–25.

Akhtar, S. (1991a). Panel report: sadomasochism in perversions. *Journal of the American Psychoanalytic Association, 39*: 741–755.

Akhtar, S. (1991b). Three fantasies related to unresolved separation–individuation: a less recognized aspect of severe character pathology.

In: S. Akhtar & H. Parens (Eds.), *Beyond the Symbiotic Orbit: Advances in Separation–Individuation Theory* (pp. 261–284). Northvale, NJ: Jason Aronson.

Akhtar, S. (1992). *Broken Structures: Severe Personality Disorders and Their Treatment*. Northvale, NJ: Jason Aronson.

Akhtar, S. (1994). Object constancy and adult psychopathology. *International Journal of Psychoanalysis, 75*: 441–455.

Akhtar, S. (1996). "Someday ..." and "if only ..." fantasies: pathological optimism and inordinate nostalgia as related forms of idealization. *Journal of American Psychoanalytic Association, 44*: 723–753.

Akhtar, S. (1999a). Review of "Internal Objects Revisited" by Joseph and Ann-Marie Sandler. *Psychoanalytic Books, 10*: 532–541.

Akhtar, S. (1999b). *Inner Torment: Living Between Conflict and Fragmentation*. Northvale, NJ: Jason Aronson.

Akhtar, S. (2000). Mental pain and the cultural ointment of poetry. *International Journal of Psychoanalysis, 81*: 229–243.

Akhtar, S. (2002). Forgiveness: origins, dynamics, psychopathology, and clinical relevance. *Psychoanalytic Quarterly, 71*: 175–212.

Akhtar, S. (2003). Things: developmental, psychopathological, and technical aspects of inanimate objects. *Canadian Journal of Psychoanalysis, 11*: 1–44.

Akhtar, S. (2005). *Objects of Our Desire*. New York: Random House.

Akhtar, S. (2007). From unmentalized xenophobia to messianic sadism: some reflections on the phenomenology of prejudice. In: H. Parens, A. Mahfouz, S. W. Twemlow, & D. E. Scharff (Eds.), *The Future of Prejudice: Psychoanalysis and the Prevention of Prejudice* (pp. 7–19). Lanham, MD: Jason Aronson.

Akhtar, S. (2009a). *Comprehensive Dictionary of Psychoanalysis*. London: Karnac.

Akhtar, S. (2009b). *The Damaged Core: Origins, Dynamics, Manifestations, and Treatment*. Lanham, MD: Jason Aronson.

Akhtar, S. (2010). Freud's *Todesangst* and Ghalib's *Ishrat-e-Qatra*: two perspectives on death. In: *The Wound of Mortality: Fear, Denial, and Acceptance of Death* (pp. 1–20). Lanham, MD: Jason Aronson.

Akhtar, S. (2011a). *Immigration and Acculturation: Mourning, Adaptation, and the Next Generation* (pp. 55–80). Lanham, MD: Jason Aronson.

Akhtar, S. (2011b). *Matters of Life and Death: Psychoanalytic Reflections*. London: Karnac.

Akhtar, S. (2012). Fear, phobia, and cowardice. In: S. Akhtar (Ed.), *Fear: A Dark Shadow Across our Life Span* (pp. 3–34). London: Karnac.

Akhtar, S. (2013a). The compulsion to betray and the need to be betrayed. In: S. Akhtar (Ed.), *Betrayal: Developmental, Literary, and Clinical Realms* (pp. 117–134). London: Karnac.

Akhtar, S. (2013b). *Psychoanalytic Listening: Methods, Limits, and Innovations* (pp. 81–101). London: Karnac.

Akhtar, S. (2014a). Revenge: an overview. In: S. Akhtar & H. Parens (Eds.). *Revenge: Narcissistic Injury, Rage, and Retaliation* (pp. 1–17). Lanham, MD: Jason Aronson.

Akhtar, S. (2014b). *After Landing*. Charlottesville, VA: Pitchstone.

Akhtar, S. (2015a). Patience. *Psychoanalytic Review, 102*: 93–122.

Akhtar, S. (2015b). Some psychoanalytic reflections on the concept of dignity. *American Journal of Psychoanalysis, 75*: (in press).

Akhtar, S. (2016). *Blood and Ink*. London: Karnac.

Akhtar, S., & Billinkoff, Z. (2011). Developmental tasks of early marriage: "Barefoot in the Park" (1967), "Raising Arizona" (1987), "The Quiet Man" (1952). *American Journal of Psychoanalysis, 71*: 110–120.

Akhtar, S., & Blue, S. (2017). The emotional impact of divorce: an overview. In: S. Akhtar (Ed.), *Divorce: Emotional Impact and Therapeutic Interventions* (pp. 1–30). Lanham, MD: Rowman & Littlefield (in press).

Altman, L. (1977). Some vicissitudes of love. *Journal of the American Psychoanalytic Association, 25*: 35–52.

Alvarez, P. (2016). Justice Ginsburg's "Ill-Advised Comment" on Donald Trump. *Atlantic Monthly,* July 14, p. 14.

Amati-Mehler, J., & Argentieri, S. (1989). Hope and hopelessness: a technical problem? *International Journal of Psychoanalysis, 70*: 295–304.

Angel, A. (1934). Einige bemerkungen uber den optimismus. *International Journal of Psychoanalysis, 20*: 191–199.

Arlow, J., & Brenner, C. (1964). *Psychoanalytic Concepts and Structural Theory*. New York: International Universities Press.

Asherman, I., Bing, J. W., & Laroche, L. (2000). Building trust across cultural boundaries. *Regulatory Affairs Focus, 13*: 21–40.

Auchincloss, E. L., & Samberg, E. (Eds.) (2012). *Psychoanalytic Terms and Concepts*. New Haven, CT: Yale University Press.

Auerhahn, N., & Laub, D. (1987). Play and playfulness in Holocaust survivors. *Psychoanalytic Study of the Child, 42*: 45–58.

Bach, S. (1977). On the narcissistic state of consciousness. *International Journal of Psychoanalysis, 58*: 209–233.

Balint, M. (1948). On genital love. *International Journal of Psychoanalysis, 29*: 34–40.

Balint, M. (1953). *Primary Love and Psychoanalytic Technique*. London: Tavistock.

Balint, M. (1968). *The Basic Fault: Therapeutic Aspects of Regression*. London: Tavistock.

Barag, G. (1949). A case of pathological jealousy. *Psychoanalytic Quarterly, 18*: 1–18.

Barnes, J. (2008). *Nothing To Be Frightened Of*. New York: Vintage.

Barnes, J. (2013). *The Sense of an Ending*. London: Vintage.

Barton, R., & Whitehead, J. (1969). The gaslight phenomenon. *Lancet, 1*: 158–1260.

Battistella, E. (2014). *The Language of Public Apology*. New York: Oxford University Press.

Begley, L. (1993). *The Man Who Was Late*. New York: Alfred Knopf.

Beguiled, The (1971). Directed by D. Siegel. Produced by Universal Pictures.

Benedek, T. (1938). Adaptation to reality in early infancy. *Psychoanalytic Quarterly, 7*: 200–214.

Benedek, T. (1977). Ambivalence, passion, and love. *Journal of the American Psychoanalytic Association, 25*: 53–79.

Bergmann, M. S. (1971). Psychoanalytic observations on the capacity to love. In: J. B. McDevitt & C. F. Settlage (Eds.), *Separation–Individuation* (pp. 15–40). New York: International Universities Press.

Bergmann, M. S. (1980). On the intrapsychic function of falling in love. *Psychoanalytic Quarterly, 49*: 56–77.

Bion, W. R. (1963). *Elements of Psychoanalysis*. London: Karnac, 1984.

Bion, W. R. (1967). Notes on memory and desire. In: *Cogitations* (pp. 380–385). London: Karnac.

Blevis, M. (2009). *Jealousy: True Stories of Love's Favorite Decoy*. New York: Other Press.

Blos, P. (1967). The second individuation process of adolescence. *Psychoanalytic Study of the Child, 22*: 162–186.

Blum, H. (1980). Paranoia and beating fantasy: psychoanalytic theory of paranoia. *Journal of the American Psychoanalytic Association, 28*: 331–361.

Blum, H. (1981). Object inconstancy and paranoid conspiracy. *Journal of the American Psychoanalytic Association, 29*: 789–813.

Borchard, D. C. (2006). *The Joy of Retirement*. New York: Amacom.

Boris, H. (1976). On hope: its nature and psychotherapy. *International Review of Psycho-Analysis, 3*: 139–150.

Bowlby, J. (1958). The nature of the child's tie to his mother. *International Journal of Psychoanalysis, 39*: 350–373.

Bowlby, J. (1960). Grief and mourning in infancy and early childhood. *Psychoanalytic Study of the Child, 15*: 9–52.

Bowlby, J. (1961). Processes of mourning. *International Journal of Psychoanalysis, 42*: 317–340.

Braunschweig, D., & Fain, M. (1971). *Eros et Anteros*. Paris: Petit Bibliotheque Payot.

Brenman, E. (1985). Cruelty and narrow-mindedness. *International Journal of Psychoanalysis, 66*: 273–281.

Brenner, C. (1955). *Elementary Textbook of Psychoanalysis*. New York: International Universities Press.

Brenner, C. (1976). *Psychoanalytic Technique and Psychic Conflict*. New York: International Universities Press.

Brontë, C. (1846). Regret. In: *Poems of Currer, Ellis, and Acton Bell* (pp. 325–326). London: Smith, Elder, 1888.

Brooke, R. (1908). Jealousy. In: *Collected Poems of R. Brooke* (p. 45). New York: Astounding Stories, 2015.

Brunswick, R. (1929). The analysis of a case of delusional jealousy. *Journal of Nervous and Mental Disease, 70*: 1–22.

Burland, J. A. (1975). Separation individuation and reconstruction in psychoanalysis. *International Journal of Psychoanalytic Psychotherapy, 4*: 303–335.

Burnham, D. L., Gladstone, A. E., & Gibson, R. W. (1969). *Schizophrenia and the Need-Fear Dilemma*. New York: International Universities Press.

Busch, F. (2004). *The Ego at the Center of Clinical Technique*. Northvale, NJ: Jason Aronson.

Buss, D. (2000). *The Dangerous Passion: Why Jealousy Is as Necessary as Love and Sex*. New York: Free Press.

Buunk, B. P., & Hupka, R. B. (1987). Cross-cultural differences in the elicitation of sexual jealousy. *Journal of Sex Research, 23*: 12–22.

Casement, P. (1991). *Learning from the Patient*. New York: Guilford Press.

Celenza, A. (2014). *Erotic Revelations: Clinical Applications and Perverse Scenarios*. New York: Routledge.

Chasseguet-Smirgel, J. (1984). *Creativity and Perversion*. New York: W. W. Norton.

Chasseguet-Smirgel, J. (1985). *The Ego-Ideal: A Psychoanalytical Essay on the Malady of the Ideal*. New York: W. W. Norton.

Chatterji, N. (1948). Paranoid jealousy. *Samiksa, 11*: 14–24.

Chimbos, P. D. (1978). *Marital Violence: A Study of Interspouse Homicide*. San Francisco, CA: R and R Associates.

Coen, S. (1987). Pathological jealousy. *International Journal of Psychoanalysis, 68*: 99–108.

Coetzee, J. M. (1998). *Boyhood*. London: Vintage.

Cooper, A. (1988). Our changing views of the therapeutic action of psychoanalysis: comparing Strachey and Loewald. *Psychoanalytic Quarterly, 57*: 15–27.

DeSteno, D. A., & Salovey, P. (1996). Genes, jealousy, and the replication of misspecified models. *Psychological Science, 7*: 376–377.

Diagnostic and Statistical Manual of Mental Disorders-V (2013). Washington, DC: American Psychiatric Publishing.

Dockterman, E. (2014). Former Virginia governor charged with accepting illegal gifts. *Time*, January 21, p. 16.

East of Eden (1955). Directed by E. Kazan. Warner Brothers production.

Edward, J. (2011). *The Sibling Relationship: A Force for Growth and Conflict.* Lanham, MD: Rowman & Littlefield.

Ehrlich, J. (2014). *Divorce and Loss: Helping Adults and Children Mourn When a Marriage Comes Apart.* Lanham, MD: Rowman & Littlefield.

Eidelberg, L. (Ed.) (1968). *The Encyclopedia of Psychoanalysis.* New York: Free Press.

Eissler, K. R. (1955). *The Psychiatrist and the Dying Patient.* New York: International Universities Press.

Ellman, S. J. (2007). Analytic trust and transference: love, healing ruptures and facilitating repairs. *Psychoanalytic Inquiry, 27*: 246–263.

Emde, R. (1991). Positive emotions for psychoanalytic theory: surprises from infancy research and new directions. *Journal of the American Psychoanalytic Association, 39S*: 5–44.

Epstein, L. (1979). Countertransference with borderline patients. In: L. Epstein & A. H. Feiner (Eds.), *Countertransference* (pp. 375–406). New York: Jason Aronson.

Erikson, E. H. (1950). *Childhood and Society.* New York: W. W. Norton, 1963.

Euripides, (circa 413 BC). *Medea.* London: Penguin Classics, 1963.

Eyes Wide Shut (1999). Directed by S. Kubrick. Warner Brothers production.

Fairbairn, W. R. D. (1952). *An Object Relations Theory of Psychoanalysis.* New York: Basic Books.

Fatal Attraction (1987). Directed by A. Lyne. Paramount Pictures production.

Fayek, A. (1981). Narcissism and the death instinct. *International Journal of Psychoanalysis, 63*: 309–322.

Fenichel, O. (1941). *Problems of Psychoanalytic Technique.* Albany, NY: Psychoanalytic Quarterly Press.

Fenichel, O. (1945). *The Psychoanalytic Theory of Neurosis.* New York: W. W. Norton.

Ferenczi, S. (1909). Introduction and transference. In: E. Mosbacher (Trans.), *First Contributions to Psychoanalysis* (pp. 35–93). London: Karnac, 1980.

Ferenczi, S. (1911). On obscene words. In: E. Jones (Trans.), *Contributions to Psycho-Analysis* (pp. 112–130). Boston, MA: Richard G. Budger, 1916.

Ferenczi, S. (1912). On the part played by homosexuality in the pathogenesis of paranoia. In: E. Mosbacher (Trans.), *First Contributions to Psychoanalysis* (pp. 154–186). London: Karnac, 1980.

Ferenczi, S. (1928). The elasticity of psychoanalytical technique. In: *Final Contributions to the Problems and Methods of Psychoanalysis* (pp. 87–101). New York: Basic Books, 1955.

Ferenczi, S. (1929). The unwelcome child and his death instinct. *International Journal of Psychoanalysis, 10*: 125–129.

Ferenczi, S. (1930). Thoughts on "pleasure in passivity". In: *Final Contributions to the Problems and Methods of Psychoanalysis* (pp. 224–227). New York: Brunner/Mazel, 1980.

Ferenczi, S. (1931). Child-analysis in the analysis of adults. *International Journal of Psychoanalysis, 12*: 468–482.

Ferenczi, S. (1933). On the confusion of tongues between adults and the child. In: *Final Contributions to the Problems and Methods of Psychoanalysis* (pp. 155–167). New York: Basic Books, 1955.

Fodor, N. (1950). Varieties of nostalgia. *Psychoanalytic Review, 37*: 25–38.

Fonagy, P., & Target, M. (1997). Attachment and reflective function: their role in self-organization. *Development and Psychopathology, 9*: 679–700.

Fox, R. (1998). The unobjectionable positive countertransference. *Journal of the American Psychoanalytic Association, 46*: 1067–1087.

Frank, A. (1969). Unrememberable and unforgettable: passive primal repression. *Psychoanalytic Study of the Child, 24*: 48–62.

Frank, K. (2004). The analyst's trust and therapeutic action. *Psychoanalytic Quarterly, 73*: 335–378.

French, T. M. (1945). The integration of social behavior. *Psychoanalytic Quarterly, 14*: 149–161.

French, T. M., & Wheeler, D. R. (1963). Hope and repudiation of hope in psycho-analytic therapy. *International Journal of Psychoanalysis, 44*: 304–316.

Freud, A. (1936). *The Ego and the Mechanisms of Defense.* New York: International Universities Press.

Freud, S. (1895). Extracts from the Fliess Papers. Draft K—the neuroses of defence. *S. E., 1*: 220–229. London: Hogarth.

Freud, S. (1897). Extracts from the Fliess Papers. Letter 75. November, 1897. *S. E., 1*: 268–271. London: Hogarth.

Freud, S. (1899a). Screen memories. *S. E., 3*: 301–323. London: Hogarth.

Freud, S. (1900a). *The Interpretation of Dreams. S. E., 4–5.* London: Hogarth.

Freud, S. (1905a). On psychotherapy. *S. E., 7*: 257–268. London: Hogarth.

Freud, S. (1905d). *Three Essays on the Theory of Sexuality. S. E., 7*: 135–243. London: Hogarth.

Freud, S. (1907a). *Delusions and Dreams in Jensen's "Gradiva". S. E., 9*: 1–96. London: Hogarth.

Freud, S. (1908b). Character and anal erotism. *S. E., 9*: 167–176. London: Hogarth.

Freud, S. (1908e). Creative writers and day-dreaming. *S. E., 9*: 141–154. London: Hogarth.

Freud, S. (1911b). Formulations on the two principles of mental functioning. *S. E., 12*: 213–226. London: Hogarth.

Freud, S. (1911c). Psycho-analytic notes on an autobiographical account of a case of paranoia. *S. E., 12*: 1–82. London: Hogarth.

Freud, S. (1912d). On the universal tendency to debasement in the sphere of love. *S. E., 11*: 178–190. London: Hogarth.

Freud, S. (1912e). Recommendations to physicians practising psychoanalysis. *S. E., 12*: 109–120. London: Hogarth.

Freud, S. (1914c). On narcissism: an introduction. *S. E., 14*: 69–102. London: Hogarth.

Freud, S. (1915a). Observations on transference-love (further recommendations on the technique of psycho-analysis, III). *S. E., 12*. London: Hogarth.

Freud, S. (1915c). Instincts and their vicissitudes. *S. E., 14*: 117–140. London: Hogarth.

Freud, S. (1915e). The unconscious. *S. E., 14*: 159–216. London: Hogarth.

Freud, S. (1917b). A childhood recollection from *Dichtung und Wahrheit*. *S. E., 17*: 145–156. London: Hogarth.

Freud, S. (1917e). Mourning and melancholia. *S. E., 14*: 237–258. London: Hogarth.

Freud, S. (1918b). From the history of an infantile neurosis. *S. E., 17*: 7–122. London: Hogarth.

Freud, S. (1919j). On the teaching of psycho-analysis in universities. *S. E., 17*: 169–173. London: Hogarth.

Freud, S. (1920g). *Beyond the Pleasure Principle. S. E., 18*: 7–64. London: Hogarth.

Freud, S. (1921c). *Group Psychology and the Analysis of the Ego. S. E., 18*: 65–144. London: Hogarth.

Freud, S. (1922b). Some neurotic mechanisms in jealousy, paranoia, and homosexuality. *S. E., 18*: 221–232. London: Hogarth.

Freud, S. (1923b). *The Ego and the Id. S. E., 19*: 12–68. London: Hogarth.

Freud, S. (1926d). *Inhibitions, Symptoms and Anxiety. S. E., 20*: 75–175. London: Hogarth.

Freud, S. (1930a). *Civilization and Its Discontents. S. E., 21*: 64–145. London: Hogarth.

Freud, S. (1932a). The acquisition and control of fire. *S. E., 22*. London: Hogarth.

Freud, S. (1933a). *New Introductory Lectures on Psycho-Analysis. S. E., 22*: 122–135. London: Hogarth.

Friedman, L. (1969). The therapeutic alliance. *International Journal of Psychoanalysis, 50*: 139–153.

Friedman, L. (2005). Is there a special psychoanalytic love? *Journal of the American Psychoanalytic Association, 53*: 349–375.

Friedman, S. (1989). Strategic reframing in a case of delusional jealousy. *Journal of Strategic and Systemic Therapies, 8*: 1–4.

Gay, P. (1988). *Freud: A Life for Our Time*. New York: W. W. Norton.

Gediman, H. (1985). Impostor, inauthenticity, and feeling fraudulent. *Journal of the American Psychoanalytic Association*, *39*: 911–936.

Gedo, J. E., & Goldberg, A. (1973). *Models of the Mind*. Chicago, IL: University of Chicago Press.

Gerrard, J. (2011). *The Impossibility of Knowing: Dilemmas of a Psychotherapist*. London: Karnac.

Gilmartin, B. G. (1986). Jealousy among the swingers. In: G. Clanton & L. G. Smith (Eds.), *Jealousy* (pp. 152–158). Lanham, MD: University Press of America.

Glover, E. (1925). Notes on oral character formations. *International Journal of Psychoanalysis*, *6*: 131–153.

Graduate, The (1967). Directed by M. Nichols. Lawrence Turman production.

Green, A. (1980). The dead mother. In: A. Weller (Trans.), *Life Narcissism, Death Narcissism* (pp. 185–221). London: Free Association.

Green, A. (1986). Réponses à des questions inconcevables. *Topique* 37: 11–30.

Greenson, R. (1958). Variations in classical psychoanalytic technique. *International Journal of Psychoanalysis*, *39*: 200–211.

Greenspan, S. (1977). The oedipal–preoedipal dilemma: a reformulation in the light of object relations theory. *International Review of Psycho-Analysis*, *6*: 612–627.

Grinker, R. (1955). Growth inertia and shame: their therapeutic implications and dangers. *International Journal of Psychoanalysis*, *36*: 267–276.

Guardian, The (2009). Howard Jacobson's top 10 novels of sexual jealousy. Wednesday, November 4. Accessed at www.theguardian.com/books/2009/nov/03/howard-jacobson-top-10–sexual-jealousy, on September 6, 2016.

Guerin, P. J., Fay, L. F., Burden, S. L., & Kautto, J. G. (1987). *The Evaluation and Treatment of Marital Conflict: a Four-Stage Approach*. New York: Basic Books.

Guntrip, H. (1969). *Schizoid Phenomena, Object Relations, and the Self*. New York: International Universities Press.

Guttman, S. A., Jones R. L., & Parrish, S. M. (Eds.) (1980). *The Concordance to the Standard edition of the Complete Psychological Works of Sigmund Freud*. Boston, MA: G. K. Hall.

Hardy, T. (1891). *Tess of the D'Urbervilles*. London: Penguin, 2003.

Hartmann, H. (1939). *Ego Psychology and the Problem of Adaptation*. D. Rapaport (Trans.). New York: International Universities Press, 1958.

Hartmann, H. (1955). Notes on the theory of sublimation. *Psychoanalytic Study of the Child*, *10*: 9–29.

Haynal, A. (1988). *The Technique at Issue: Controversies in Psychoanalysis from Freud and Ferenczi to Michael Balint*. E. Holder (Trans.). London: Karnac.

Haynal, A. (2002). *Disappearing and Reviving: Sandor Ferenczi in the History of Psychoanalysis*. London: Karnac.

Heimann, P. (1950). On countertransference. *International Journal of Psychoanalysis, 31*: 81–84.

Heller, J. (1966). *Something Happened*. New York: Charles Scribner's Sons, 1974.

Hemingway, E. (1936). The Snows of Kilimanjaro. In: *The Complete Short Stories of Ernest Hemingway: The Finca Vigia Edition* (pp. 56–87). New York: Charles Scribner's Sons.

Hoffer, E. (1974). Long live shame. *The New York Times*, D-4, October 18.

Hoffman, I. (1992). Some practical implications of a social constructivist view of the psychoanalytic situation. *Psychoanalytic Dialogues, 2*: 287–304.

Horowitz, M. (1975). Sliding meanings: a defense against threat in narcissistic personalities. *International Journal of Psychoanalytic Psychotherapy, 4*: 167–180.

Isaacs, K., Alexander, J., & Haggard, E. (1963). Faith, trust, and gullibility. *International Journal of Psychoanalysis, 44*: 461–469.

Jacobson, E. (1971). *Depression*. New York: International Universities Press.

Jaques, E. (2005). On trust, good, and evil. *International Journal of Applied Psychoanalytic Studies, 2*: 396–403.

Jones, E. (1929). Jealousy. In: *Papers on Psychoanalysis* (pp. 282–295). London: Bailliere, Tindall & Cox, 1950.

Jones, E. (1955). *The Life and Work of Sigmund Freud, Vol. II*. New York: Basic Books.

Jung, C. G. (1933). *Modern Man in Search of a Soul*. New York: Harcourt Brace Jovanovich.

Kahneman, D., & Tversky, A. (1982). The psychology of preferences. *Scientific American, 246*: 160–173.

Katon, A. (1961). Some thoughts about the role of verbalization in early childhood. *Psychoanalytic Study of the Child, 16*: 184–188.

Kavaler-Adler, S. (2004). Anatomy of regret: the critical turn towards love and creativity in the transforming schizoid personality. *American Journal of Psychoanalysis, 64*: 39–76.

Kelman, H. (1945). Neurotic pessimism. *Psychoanalytic Review, 32*: 419–448.

Kernberg, O. F. (1974a). Barriers to falling and remaining in love. In: *Object Relations Theory and Clinical Psychoanalysis* (pp. 185–213). New York: Jason Aronson, 1976.

Kernberg, O. F. (1974b). Mature love: prerequisites and characteristics. *Journal of the American Psychoanalytic Association, 22*: 743–768.

Kernberg, O. F. (1975). *Borderline Conditions and Pathological Narcissism.* New York: Jason Aronson.

Kernberg, O. F. (1980). *Internal World and External Reality: Object Relations Theory Applied.* New York: Jason Aronson.

Kernberg, O. F. (1984). *Severe Personality Disorders: Psychotherapeutic Strategies.* New Haven, CT: Yale University Press.

Kernberg, O. F. (1991a). Sadomasochism, sexual excitement, and perversion. *Journal of the American Psychoanalytic Association, 39*: 333–362.

Kernberg, O. F. (1991b). Aggression and love in the relationship of the couple. *Journal of the American Psychoanalytic Association, 39*: 486–511.

Kernberg, O. F. (1992). *Aggression in Personality Disorders and Perversions.* New Haven, CT: Yale University Press.

Kernberg, O. F. (1993). The couple's constructive and destructive superego functions. *Journal of the American Psychoanalytic Association, 41*: 653–677.

Kernberg, O. F. (1995). *Love Relations: Normality and Pathology.* New Haven, CT: Yale University Press.

Khan, M. M. R. (1966). Phobic and counterphobic mechanisms and separation anxiety in schizoid character formation. In: *The Privacy of the Self* (pp. 69–81). New York: International Universities Press, 1974.

Kilborne, B. (2005). Shame conflicts and tragedy in "The Scarlet Letter". *Journal of the American Psychoanalytic Association, 53*: 465–483.

Killingmo, B. (1989). Conflict and deficit: implications for technique. *International Journal of Psychoanalysis, 70*: 65–79.

Kitayama, S. (2004). Cross cultural varieties in experiencing affect. In: S. Akhtar & H. Blum (Eds.), *The Language of Emotions* (pp. 33–48). Northvale, NJ: Jason Aronson.

Kitayama, S. (2007). *Gekitekina Seishinbunseki-Nyuumon: A Dramatic Introduction to Psycho-Analysis.* Tokyo: Misuzu Shobo.

Kjellqvist, E. (1993). *Red and White: On Shame and Shamelessness.* Stockholm: Carlsson.

Klein, M. (1927). Criminal tendencies in normal children. In: *Love, Guilt and Reparation and Other Works 1921–1945* (pp. 170–185). New York: Free Press, 1975.

Klein, M. (1928). Early stages of the Oedipus conflict. In: *Love, Guilt and Reparation and Other Works 1921–1945* (pp. 186–198). New York: Free Press, 1975.

Klein, M. (1930). The importance of symbol-formation in the development of the ego. *International Journal of Psychoanalysis, 11*: 24–39.

Klein, M. (1935). A contribution to the psychogenesis of manic depressive states. In: *Love, Guilt and Reparation and Other Works 1921–1945* (pp. 262–289). New York: Free Press, 1975.

Klein, M. (1940). Mourning and its relation to manic depressive states. In: *Love, Guilt and Reparation and Other Works 1921–1945* (pp. 344–369). New York: Free Press, 1975.

Klein, M. (1946). Notes on some schizoid mechanisms. In: *Envy and Gratitude and Other Works 1946–1963* (pp. 1–24). New York: Free Press, 1975.

Klein, M. (1952). Some theoretical conclusions regarding the emotional life of the infant. In: *Envy and Gratitude and Other Works 1946–1963* (pp. 61–93). New York: Free Press, 1975.

Klein, M. (1957). Envy and gratitude. In: *Envy and Gratitude and Other Works 1946–1963* (pp. 176–235). New York: Free Press, 1975.

Kleiner, J. (1970). On nostalgia. *Bulletin of the Philadelphia Association for Psychoanalysis, 20*: 11–30.

Kohut, H. (1966). Forms and transformation of narcissism. *Journal of the American Psychoanalytic Association, 14*: 243–272.

Kohut, H. (1971). *The Analysis of the Self. A Systematic Approach to the Psychoanalytic Treatment of Narcissistic Personality Disorders.* New York: International Universities Press.

Kohut, H. (1972). Thoughts on narcissism and narcissistic rage. *Psychoanalytic Study of the Child, 27*: 360–400.

Kohut, H. (1977). *The Restoration of the Self.* New York: International Universities Press.

Kramer, S., & Akhtar, S. (1988). The developmental context of internalized preoedipal object relations: clinical applications of Mahler's theory of symbiosis and separation–individuation. *Psychoanalytic Quarterly, 57*: 547–576.

Krause, R. (2009). Commentary. In: S. Akhtar (Ed.), *Good Feelings: Psychoanalytic Reflections on Positive Emotions and Attitudes* (pp. 203–212). London: Karnac.

Kretschmer, E. (1925). *Physique and Character.* W. J. H. Sprott (Trans.). New York: Harcourt Brace.

Kris, E. (1956). On some vicissitudes of insight in psychoanalysis. *International Journal of Psychoanalysis, 37*: 445–455.

Landman, J. (1993). *Regret.* New York: Oxford University Press.

Langs, R. (2004). Death anxiety and the emotion-processing mind. *Psychoanalytic Psychology, 21*: 31–53.

Lansky, M. (1991). Shame and the problem of suicide: a family systems perspective. *British Journal of Psychotherapy, 7*: 230–242.

Lansky, M. (1994). Shame: contemporary psychoanalytic perspectives. *Journal of the American Academy of Psychoanalysis, 22*: 433–441.

Lansky, M. (1999). Shame and the idea of a central affect. *Psychoanalytic Inquiry, 19*: 347–361.

Lansky, M. (2000). Shame dynamics in the psychotherapy of the patient with PTSD: a viewpoint. *Journal of the American Academy of Psychoanalysis, 28*: 133–146.

Lansky, M. (2003a). Shame conflicts as dream instigators: wish fulfillment and the ego ideal in dream dynamics. *American Journal of Psychoanalysis, 63*: 357–364.

Lansky, M. (2003b). The "incompatible idea" revisited: the oft-invisible ego-ideal and shame dynamics. *American Journal of Psychoanalysis, 63*: 365–376.

Lansky, M. (2004). Trigger and screen: shame conflicts and the dynamics of instigation in Freud's dreams. *Journal of the American Psychoanalytic Association, 32*: 441–469.

Lansky, M. (2005). Hidden shame. *Journal of the American Psychoanalytic Association, 53*: 864–890.

Lansky, M. (2007). Unbearable shame, splitting, and forgiveness in the resolution of vengefulness. *Journal of the American Psychoanalytic Association, 55*: 571–593.

Lapierre, D., & Collins, L. (1975). *Freedom at Midnight.* New York: Simon & Schuster.

Laplanche, J., & Pontalis, J.-B. (1973). *The Language of Psychoanalysis.* New York: W. W. Norton.

Lasch, C. (1971). *The Culture of Narcissism: American Life in an Age of Diminishing Expectations.* New York: W. W. Norton.

Laura (1944). Directed by O. Preminger. Twentieth Century Fox production.

Lax, R. F. (2008). Becoming really old: the indignities. *Psychoanalytic Quarterly, 77*: 835–857.

Levin, R. (1998). Faith, paranoia, and trust in the psychoanalytic relationship. *Journal of the American Academy of Psychoanalysis, 26*: 553–572.

Levin, S. (1967). Some metapsychological considerations on the differentiation between shame and guilt. *International Journal of Psychoanalysis, 48*: 267–276.

Levinson, D., Darrow, C., Klein, E., Levinson, M., & McKee, B. (1978). *Seasons of a Man's Life.* New York: Alfred Knopf.

Lewin, R., & Schulz, C. (1992). *Losing and Fusing: Borderline Transitional Object and Self Relations.* Northvale, NJ: Jason Aronson.

Lewin, S. (2011). Parallel identification: a shield against the assault of traumatic jealousy. *Psychoanalytic Dialogues, 21*: 551–570.

Lewontin, R. (1968). Honest Jim Watson's "big think" DNA. *Chicago Sunday Times, Book Week, 25*: 1–2.

Lidz, T. (1968). *The Person: His and Her Development Throughout the Life Cycle.* New York: Basic Books (revised edn.), 1983.

Loewald, H. (1960). On the therapeutic action of psychoanalysis. *Journal of the American Psychoanalytic Association, 41*: 16–33.

Loewald, H. (1970). Psychoanalytic theory and psychoanalytic process. *Psychoanalytic Study of the Child, 25*: 45–68.

Lowenfeld, H. (1976). Notes on shamelessness. *Psychoanalytic Quarterly, 45*: 62–72.

Mahler, M. S., Pine, F., & Bergman, A. (1975). *The Psychological Birth of the Human Infant: Symbiosis and Individuation*. New York: Basic Books.

Masson, J. M. (1985). *The Complete Letters of Sigmund Freud to Wilhelm Fliess*. Cambridge, MA: Harvard University Press.

McGinniss, J. (1983). *Fatal Vision*. New York: Penguin.

McLaughlin, J. (1992). Non-verbal behaviors in the analytic situation. In: S. Kramer & S. Akhtar (Eds.), *When the Body Speaks: Psychological Meanings in Kinetic Clues* (pp. 131–161). Northvale, NJ: Jason Aronson.

Mead, M. (1931). Jealousy: primitive and civilized. In: S. D. Schmalhausen & V. F. Calverton (Eds.), *Women's Coming of Age* (pp. 35–48). New York: Horace Liveright.

Meissner, W. (1969). Notes on the psychology of faith. *Journal of Religion and Health, 8*: 47–75.

Menninger, K. (1959). *A Psychoanalyst's World*. New York: Viking.

Merriam-Webster's Collegiate Dictionary (1998). Baltimore, MD: Williams & Wilkins.

Mildred Pierce (1945). Directed by T. Garnett. Warner Brothers production.

Miller, F. N. (1985). Hopelessness: a narcissistic resistance. *Modern Psychoanalysis, 10*: 65–79.

Mish, F. C. (Ed.) (1993). *Merriam Webster's Collegiate Dictionary (9th Edition)*. Springfield, MA: Merriam Webster Press.

Mitchell, S. (1993). *Hope and Dread in Psychoanalysis*. New York: Basic Books.

Mollon, P. (2002). *Shame and Jealousy: The Hidden Turmoils*. London: Karnac.

Moore, B., & Fine, B. (Eds.) (1968). *A Glossary of Psychoanalytic Terms and Concepts*. New York: American Psychoanalytic Association.

Moore, B., & Fine, B. (Eds.) (1990). *Psychoanalytic Terms and Concepts*. New Haven, CT: Yale University Press.

Morrison, A. (1989). *Shame: The Underside of Narcissism*. Hillsdale, NJ: Analytic Press.

Mullen, P. E. (1996). Editorial: jealousy and the emergence of violence and intimidating behaviors. *Criminal Behavior and Mental Health, 6*: 199–205.

Neri, C. (2005). What is the function of faith and trust in psychoanalysis? *International Journal of Psychoanalysis, 86*: 79–97.

Neubauer, P. (1982). Rivalry, envy, and jealousy. *Psychoanalytic Study of the Child, 37*: 121–142.

Niagara (1953). Directed by H. Hathaway. Twentieth Century Fox production.

Niazi, M. (1986). Humesha der kar deta hoon main. In: *Tez Hava Aur Tanha Phool* (p. 32). Islamabad, Pakistan: Dost Publications, 2008.

Niederland, W. (1968). Clinical observations on the "survivor syndrome". *International Journal of Psychoanalysis, 49*: 313–315.

Nietzsche, F. (1886). *Beyond Good and Evil*. New York: Dover Edition, 1961.

Nietzsche, F. (1905). *Thus Spake Zarathustra*. New York: Modern Library Series, 1955.

Nunberg, H., & Federn, E. (1962). *Minutes of the Vienna Psychoanalytic Society: Volume I: 1906–1908*. New York: International Universities Press.

Okano, K. (1998). *Psychoanalysis of Shame and Narcissism*. Tokyo: Isawaki Gakujutsu Shuppansha.

Ortega, M. J. (1959). Delusions of jealousy. *Psychoanalytic Review, 46D*: 102–103.

Pam, A., & Pearson, J. (1994). The geometry of the eternal triangle. *Family Process, 33*: 175–190.

Pao, P.-N. (1969). Pathological jealousy. *Psychoanalytic Quarterly, 38*: 616–638.

Paul, L., & Galloway, J. (1994). Sexual jealousy: gender differences in response to partner and rival. *Aggressive Behavior, 20*: 203–211.

Pierloot, R. A. (1988). Impersonal objects in morbid jealousy. *International Review of Psycho-Analysis, 15*: 293–305.

Piers, G., & Singer, M. (1953). *Shame and Guilt: A Psychoanalytic and a Cultural Study*. New York: W. W. Norton.

Pine, F. (1997). *Diversity and Direction in Psychoanalytic Technique*. New Haven, CT: Yale University Press.

Pines, A. M. (1983). Sexual jealousy as a cause of violence. Paper presented at the annual convention of the American Psychological Association, Anaheim, CA.

Pines, A. M. (1998). *Romantic Jealousy: Causes, Symptoms, Cures*. New York: Routledge.

Pinta, E. (1979). Pathological tolerance. *American Journal of Psychiatry, 135*: 698–701.

Pinter, H. (1975). *No Man's Land*. New York: Grove Press.

Platt, C. (2015). The dialectic of shame in cross-cultural therapeutic encounters. In: S. Akhtar (Ed.), *Shame: Developmental, Cultural, and Clinical Realms* (pp. 141–160). London: Karnac.

Pollock, G. H. (1971). On time, death, and immortality. *Psychoanalytic Quarterly, 40*: 435–466.

Potamianou, A. (1992). *Un bouclier dans l'economie des etats l'espoir*. Paris: Presses Universitaires de France.

Proust, M. (1913). *Remembrance of Things Past*. Ware, UK: Wordsworth Editions, 2006.

Racker, H. (1968). *Transference and Countertransference*. New York: International Universities Press.

Riviere, J. (1932). Jealousy as a mechanism of defense. *International Journal of Psychoanalysis, 13*: 414–429.

Robbe-Grillet, A. (1957). *La Jealousie*. Paris: Editions de Minuit, 1980.

Roland, A. (1988). *In Search of Self in India and Japan*. Princeton, NJ: Princeton University Press.

Rosenfeld, H. (1971). A clinical approach to the psychoanalytic theory of the life and death instincts: an investigation into aggressive aspects of narcissism. *International Journal of Psychoanalysis, 52*: 169–178.

Ross, J. M. (2003). Preconscious defense analysis, memory, and structural change. *International Journal of Psychoanalysis, 84*: 59–76.

Rycroft, C. (1960). The analysis of a paranoid personality. *International Journal of Psychoanalysis, 41*: 59–69.

Rycroft, C. (1968). *A Critical Dictionary of Psychoanalysis*. London: Penguin, 1972.

Sandler, J. (1976). Countertransference and role-responsiveness. *International Review of Psychoanalysis, 3*: 43–47.

Sandler, J., & Sandler, A.-M. (1998). *Internal Objects Revisited*. London: Karnac.

Sanguinetti, V. (2017). Governments and public trust. In: S. Akhtar (Ed.), *Mistrust: Developmental, Cultural, and Clinical Realms* (pp. 61–81). London: Karnac.

Schafer, R. (1983). *The Analytic Attitude*. London: Karnac.

Schmale, A. H., Jr. (1964). A genetic view of affects with special reference to the genesis of helplessness and hopelessness. *Psychoanalytic Study of the Child, 19*: 287–310.

Schmidberg, M. (1953). Some aspects of jealousy and of feeling hurt. *Psychoanalytic Review, 40*: 1–16.

Searles, H. F. (1977). The development of mature hope in the patient-therapist relationship. In: *Countertransference and Related Subjects: Selected Papers* (pp. 479–502). New York: International Universities Press, 1979.

Semel, V. (1990). Confrontations with hopelessness: psychoanalytic treatment of the older woman. *Modern Psychoanalysis, 12*: 215–224.

Sen, A. (1999). *Development as Freedom*. New York: Anchor.

Settlage, C. F. (1992). Psychoanalytic observations on adult development in life and in the therapeutic relationship. *Psychoanalytic Contemporary Thought, 15*: 349–374.

Settlage, C. F. (1993). Therapeutic process and developmental process in the restructuring of object and self constancy. *Journal of the American Psychoanalytic Association, 41*: 473–492.

Shackelford, T. K., Buss, D. M., & Bennett, K. (2002). Forgiveness or breakup: Sex differences in responses to a partner's infidelity. *Cognition and Emotion, 16*: 299–307.

Shaffer, P. (1979). *Amadeus*. London: National Theatre, November 2.

Shakespeare, W. (1603). *Othello*. Oxford: Oxford University Press, 2009.

Shapiro, D. (1965). *Neurotic Styles*. New York: Basic Books.

Shneidman, E. (2008). *A Commonsense Book of Death*. Lanham, MD: Rowman & Littlefield.

Siedenberg, R. (1952a). Fidelity and jealousy: socio-cultural considerations. *Psychoanalytic Review, 54D*: 27–52.

Siedenberg, R. (1952b). Jealousy: the wish. *Psychoanalytic Review, 39*: 345–353.

Sievers, B. (2003). Against all reason: trusting in trust. *Organizational and Social Dynamics, 3*: 19–39.

Slochower, H. (1984). Hope beyond hopelessness. *American Imago, 41*: 237–243.

Sonnenberg, S. M. (1972). A special form of survivor syndrome. *Psychoanalytic Quarterly, 41*: 58–62.

Spero, M. H. (1984). Shame: an object-relational formulation. *Psychoanalytic Study of the Child, 39*: 259–282.

Spielman, P. M. (1971). Envy and jealousy: an attempt at clarification. *Psychoanalytic Quarterly, 40*: 59–82.

Spitz, R. (1946). Anaclitic depression: An inquiry into the genesis of psychiatric conditions in early childhood. *Psychoanalytic Study of the Child, 2*: 313–342.

Spitz, R. (1960). Discussion of Dr John Bowlby's paper (Grief and mourning in infancy). *Psychoanalytic Study of the Child, 15*: 85–94.

Stanton, A. H. (1978). Personality disorders. In: A. M. Nicholi (Ed.), *The Harvard Guide to Modern Psychiatry* (pp. 283–295). Cambridge, MA: Harvard University Press.

Steiner, J. (1993). *Psychic Retreats: Pathological Organizations in Psychotic, Neurotic and Borderline Patients*. London: Routledge.

Sterba, E. (1940). Homesickness and the mother's breast. *Psychiatric Quarterly, 14*: 701–707.

Stone, L. (1961). *The Psychoanalytic Situation*. New York: International Universities Press.

Strachey, J. (1934). The nature of the therapeutic action of psychoanalysis. *International Journal of Psychoanalysis, 50*: 275–292.

Strenger, C. (1989). The classic and romantic visions in psychoanalysis. *International Journal of Psychoanalysis, 70*: 595–610.

Strode, W. (1620). On jealousy. In: T. Frazer (Ed.), *Selected Poems of William Strode*. Exeter, UK: Shearsman, 2001.

Suddenly Last Summer (1959). Directed by J. Mankiewicz. Columbia Pictures production.

Symonds, M. (1968). Disadvantaged children growing in a climate of hopelessness and despair. *American Journal of Psychoanalysis, 28*: 15–22.

Tagore, R. (1910). Miser. In: S. K. Das (Ed.), *English Writings of Rabindranath Tagore*, Volume I: Poems (p. 58). New Delhi: Sahitya Akademi, 2004.

Tagore, R. (1921). Question. In: W. Radicle (Ed.), *Selected Poems of Rabindranath Tagore* (p. 96). London: Penguin, 1994.

Takahashi, D. (2014). Tom Perkins apologizes for comparing the rich to the Jewish victims of the Nazis. *venturebeat.com/2014/01/27*, accessed on November 5, 2016.

Thalberg, I. (1963). Remorse. *Mind, 73*: 545–555.

Tobak, M. (1989). Lying and the paranoid personality [letter to editor]. *American Journal of Psychiatry, 146*: 125.

Tolstoy, L. (1889). The Kreutzer Sonata. In: *The Kreutzer Sonata and Other Short Stories* (pp. 64–152). Mineola, NY: Dover, 1993.

Varvin, S., & Volkan, V. (Eds.) (2005). *Violence or Dialogue?: Psychoanalytic Insights on Terror and Terrorism*. London: International Psychoanalytical Association.

Volkan, V. (1999). Psychoanalysis and diplomacy: I. Individual and large group identity. *Journal of Applied Psychoanalytic Studies, 1*: 29–45.

Volkan, V. (2004). *Blind Trust: Large Groups and Their Leaders in Times of Crises and Terror*. Charlottesville, VA: Pitchstone.

Volkan, V. (2006). *Killing in the Name of Identity: A Study of Bloody Conflicts*. Charlottesville, VA: Pitchstone.

Voltaire (1759). *Candide*. R. Pierson (Trans.). New York: Oxford University Press, 1955.

Waelder, R. (1936). The principle of multiple function: observations on multiple determination. *Psychoanalytic Quarterly, 41*: 283–290.

Wallerstein, J., Lewis, J., & Blakeslee, S. (2000). *The Unexpected Legacy of Divorce: The 25 Year Landmark Study*. New York: Hyperion.

Weigert, E. (1959). Rediscovery of trust. *American Journal of Psychoanalysis, 9*: 33–36.

Weiss, E. (1934). Bodily pain and mental pain. *International Journal of Psychoanalysis, 15*: 1–13.

Weissman, A. D. (1972). *On Dying and Denying*. New York: Behavioral Publications.

Werman, D. (1977). Normal and pathological nostalgia. *Journal of the American Psychoanalytic Association, 25*: 387–398.

Wheelis, A. (1971). The league of death. In: *The Illusionless Man* (pp. 57–95). New York: Harper Colophon.

Wheelis, A. (1975). *On Not Knowing How to Live*. New York: Harper & Row.

Wheelis, A. (1994). *The Way Things Are*. Fort Worth, TX: Baskerville.

White, G. L., & Devine, K. (1991). Romantic jealousy: therapists' perception of causes, consequences and treatment. In: G. L. White & P. E. Mullen (Eds.), *Jealousy: Theory, Research, and Clinical Strategies* (pp. 244–264). New York: Guilford Press.

White, G. L., & Mullen, P. E. (Eds.) (1989). *Jealousy: Theory, Research, and Clinical Strategies*. New York: Guilford Press.

Winnicott, D. W. (1952). Psychosis and child care. In: *Collected Papers: Through Paediatrics to Psychoanalysis* (pp. 243–255). London: Hogarth, 1958.

Winnicott, D. W. (1953). Transitional objects and transitional phenomena. *International Journal of Psychoanalysis, 34*: 89–97.

Winnicott, D. W. (1956). The antisocial tendency. In: *Collected Papers: Through Paediatrics to Psychoanalysis* (pp. 306–316). New York: Basic Books, 1958.

Winnicott, D. W. (1960a). The theory of parent–infant relationship. *International Journal of Psychoanalysis, 41*: 585–595.

Winnicott, D. W. (1960b). Ego distortion in terms of true and false self. In: *The Maturational Processes and the Facilitating Environment* (pp. 140–152). New York: International Universities Press, 1965.

Winnicott, D. W. (1963). Morals and education. In: *The Maturational Processes and the Facilitating Environment* (pp. 93–105). New York: International Universities Press, 1965.

Winokur, G. (1977). Delusional disorder. *Comprehensive Psychiatry, 18*: 511–521.

Wisdom, J. O. (1976). Jealousy in a twelve-month-old boy. *International Review of Psycho-Analysis, 3*: 365–368.

Wurmser, L. (1981). *The Mask of Shame*. Baltimore, MD: Johns Hopkins University Press.

Wurmser, L., & Jarass, H. (2007). Pathological jealousy: the perversion of love. In: L. Wurmser & H. Jarass (Eds.), *Jealousy and Envy: New Views about Two Powerful Emotions* (pp. 1–24). New York: Analytic Press.

Wurmser, L., & Jarass, H. (Eds.) (2008). *Jealousy and Envy: New Views about Two Powerful Emotions*. New York: Analytic Press.

Yuki, M., Maddux, W. W., Brewer, M. B., & Takemura, K. (2005). Cross-cultural differences in relationship and group-based trust. *Personality and Social Psychology Bulletin, 31*: 48–62.

INDEX